WAR ON WHEELS

DUKW1. (RLC Museum)

WAR ON WHEELS

THE MECHANISATION OF THE BRITISH ARMY IN THE SECOND WORLD WAR

PHILIP HAMLYN WILLIAMS

The History Press

First published 2016

The History Press
The Mill, Brimscombe Port
Stroud, Gloucestershire, GL5 2QG
www.thehistorypress.co.uk

British Library Cataloguing in Publication Data.
A catalogue record for this book is available from the British Library.

ISBN 978 0 7509 6623 8

Typesetting and origination by The History Press
Printed in India

CONTENTS

PREFACE

As a small boy in the 1950s, I knew that my father had done something 'important' in the war. I knew that my mother had been his PA and had kept scrapbooks, albums of the period, but it wasn't until some five years after my mother's death that I actually looked at what was inside those albums. The albums are referred to in the Notes as NMP albums. What I found were newspaper cuttings, photographs, speeches and diaries that together gave an outline of how the British Army was mechanised in the Second World War. My father, Major General Sir Leslie ('Bill') Williams, had led the organisation that supplied the army with its vehicles and fighting materiel: the Royal Army Ordnance Corps (RAOC).

Many books have been written on the Second World War, its battles, its vehicles and the achievements of its regiments and corps. This book does not attempt to repeat these; rather, it takes the narrative from the albums and, drawing on accounts of the motor industry and marking key events from the war, seeks to tell the story of how mechanisation was achieved. Importantly, because the albums included many newspaper cuttings about the ordinary men and women who did the work, it also gives voice to some of their personal stories. In a book of this length it is not possible to tell the whole story; in particular, I have received more individual accounts since the book went to the publishers. I have set up a website, www. waronwheels.org, to be a place where these, and other stories that the book prompts, can be recorded.

An astonishing number of people were involved: some 250,000 soldiers, Auxiliary Territorial Service (ATS) personnel and civilians in depots around Britain, but also in the furthest reaches of the Empire, along with countless volunteers, from members of Women's Institutes to schoolchildren and firemen on standby. A few of the depots were purpose built and massive, but others were set up in all manner of factory buildings, even hunt kennels and huge underground caves.

It wasn't plain sailing. The experience of the British Expeditionary Force (BEF) left the army stunned by the speed of mechanised warfare. A vast amount of equipment was left behind and had to be replaced.

The British motor industry rose to the challenge, but in the process created a storeman's nightmare with so many different models to supply and maintain. The Desert War and Italy provided yet more lessons, but on D-Day all was prepared and the army had been truly and effectively mechanised.

The Far East was not a postscript. Many of those involved with mechanisation were taken prisoners of war on the surrender of Singapore and Hong Kong and, later, extensive preparations were made for a long and gruelling land war against Japan that eventually never took place.

It would never be repeated.

This book would not have been possible had not my mother painstakingly compiled the incredibly detailed albums of my father's work in the Second World War. I thank her for this. I would like to thank my father for retaining, in his papers, material which shed so much light on events.

Thanks also to Gareth Mears, archivist at the Royal Logistics Corps (RLC) Museum, for all his help in locating material from the RAOC archive. Nevertheless, the responsibility for the contents rests with me as author. I am indebted to the National Archive; the Imperial War Museum (IWM), not least for their recorded interviews of service men and women; the Tank Museum; the National Army Museum; the National Motor Museum and the British Library; but more so to those many service men and women who kept a record of what they did or what they experienced in those dark war years. Thanks to those who spoke to me of their own, or of their parents' experiences. Thanks to Amy Rigg and colleagues of my publishers, The History Press, for backing the book and for all their patience and care.

Special thanks go to my wife, Maggie, and my family and friends for all their encouragement and support in what has been a labour of love.

Final thanks go to my father and my mother and the thousands who worked with them to do the incredible work that this book describes.

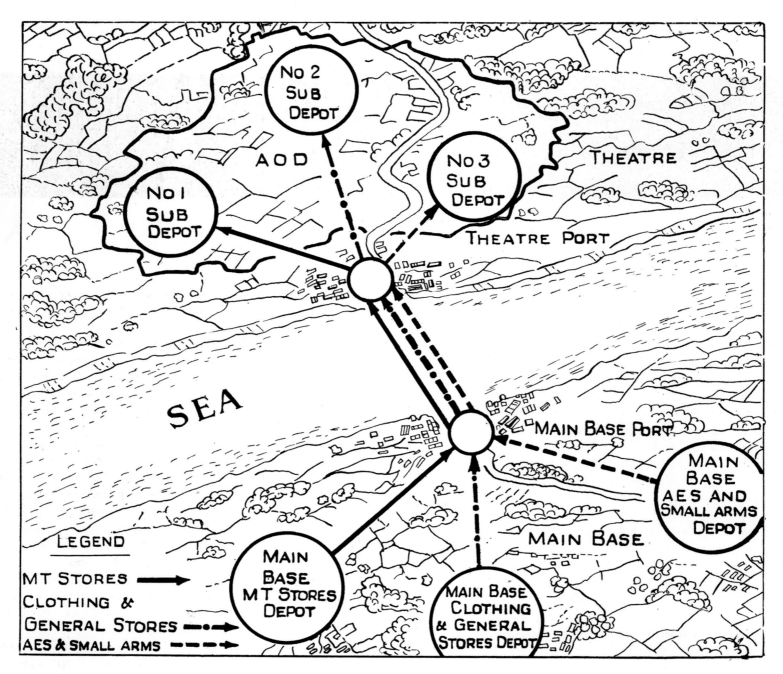

RAOC supplies map. (RLC Museum)

THE BEGINNING

Had you been a passenger on the omnibus from Nottingham Station to the little village of Chilwell on a wet November morning in 1934, you may have seen a tall, heavily built soldier fidgeting as he sat, his eyes scanning all that they passed. In his pocket was the letter from the War Office instructing him to visit the site of a former shell-filling factory. In his mind there could well have been wild imaginings: a fully mechanised army, light years from that which he had experienced in the four dark years of the Great War. He had been asked to see whether the site could be right for the first Royal Army Ordnance Corps depot specifically for motor transport (MT) and, if so, to work out how he would create it.[1]

In the late 1920s the War Office had begun to explore just what a mechanised army might look like by setting up an experimental armoured force. However, during the Depression this came to nothing as the government sought to conserve resources and set its face against rearmament. The Royal Army Ordnance Corps (RAOC) had suffered more than most. Now things were going to change.[2]

The role of the RAOC was to supply fighting troops with everything they needed, except for food and fuel. It was the Cinderella of the army and it is probably safe to say that it was regarded as a corps of storemen, who were never to confront an enemy and would seldom leave the safety of the warehouse. This was reflected in the staffing, which was overwhelmingly civilian, and even the soldiers were not regarded as combatant troops. The army nickname for ordnance men was 'blanket stackers'. If the corps itself had suffered, so too had the army's equipment: there were no more than 4,000 vehicles for the whole service and most of those were old and unreliable, with few in the corps able to maintain them – the corps had only twenty-five drivers.[3]

Bill Williams was a temporary lieutenant colonel and had spent six years at Catterick in Yorkshire, a depot that was gaining a reputation for forward thinking in the field of mechanisation. In the aftermath of the Great War, his corps had had the job of clearing up after the devastation of the trenches and Bill had been the last officer to leave, bringing back the final pieces of equipment from the Rhine.

He already had a passion for motor vehicles. He had been issued with a motorcycle in his role as machine gun officer in the Suffolk Regiment, which he joined at the outbreak of the Great War, but he later gave it up when he and his bike met a wall at speed. Then, when he was stationed on Gibraltar in the early 1920s, as ordnance officer for both the army and the navy, a US naval officer whom he'd met arranged to ship over a Ford Model T. This became his pride and joy. At Catterick, his most treasured possession was a Sunbeam. In 1937 he took delivery of a silver grey Jaguar, which he would have serviced at their factory in Coventry. There he got to know a man called Dan Warren who then worked for SS Cars to which the name Jaguar was later added. Dan, like so many other talented motor men whom Bill met, would have a significant part to play in the story that followed.[4]

Bill's passion for motor cars was shared by a great many, mostly young men. Car ownership had spread among the middle classes.[5] It wasn't just work, cars were about leisure, but above all about speed. It has been said that Battle

Brigadier Bill Williams at his desk at COD Chilwell.

Evacuation of the British Army of the Rhine in 1928.

of Britain pilots were only as effective as they were because a great many had driven cars at speed and so had developed quick reactions.[6] Relatively widespread car ownership was the result of innovative manufacturers who knew how to tempt their customers. It also produced a network of repair garages around the country staffed by men rapidly developing skills as motor mechanics.

Some years later, Bill recalled his first impressions of Chilwell:

> My first view of this magnificent depot was of a square mile of junk, weeds, railway lines, one messenger, one civilian artificer with a few maintenance men employed mainly on the heavy guns mounted on railway mountings.[7]

The site may have been derelict, but it was in the right place: good road and rail links, a plentiful supply of staff, but above all close to Coventry. On the outskirts of Nottingham, Chilwell was near the motor industry and that held the key – wars in the middle of the twentieth century would be fought on wheels. The derelict factory, which had been the largest shell-filling factory in Britain, had supplied most of the ammunition fired on the Western Front. It had been created by Viscount Chetwynd, a man of great vision, but in

1918 it suffered a disastrous explosion which cost the lives of 134 munition workers and rendered most of the site useless. After the war, what remained of the site became a general ordnance depot until it closed in 1926, except for use for Territorial Army camps. One of Bill's first acts on taking command was to put in place a tradition of honouring those munition workers on each Armistice Day.[8]

Albert Mears, whose aunt had worked in the factory during the Great War, remembered playing in the deserted depot:

> Part of the game was to get inside the depot without being spotted by the watchman; once inside it was boy's paradise. The old mill buildings with their wood runways still stood as did the Press Houses, but the whole area was covered in brambles. The buildings were still painted in camouflage colours and many old canvas buckets, used for carrying the powder, lay about the place but this all changed when builders came. Later when war broke out and we lads joined the Sherwood Foresters our Instructors always said we were better at avoiding the sentries than the rest – we reckoned our journeys into the depot had stood us in good stead.[9]

Bill Williams had been born in 1891 and on his father's death in 1906 had had no choice but to leave school. He worked first at an insurance office before he grasped the opportunity to trade in East Africa and then plant rubber in Malaya, before returning to work with the *Overseas Daily Mirror*. Like many of his contemporaries he joined the Territorials, in his case, the London Scottish. On the declaration of war in August 1914 he joined the Suffolk Regiment but soon transferred to the Army Ordnance Corps (AOC) as a bomb disposal officer.

He was posted to France and in 1915 at a railhead at St Venant, in the maelstrom of the Great War, he met Dickie Richards, who would become his great friend and rival. Dickie, just one year Bill's junior, then commanded an ammunition train and Bill was the ordnance officer attached to the 19th Division. They both won an MC (Military Cross). They were leaders; Bill was perhaps the more organised and visionary, and Dickie, in Bill's words, 'a law unto himself' who later, in the Middle East, earned for the corps a reputation for 'getting things done'.[10] They would go on to spearhead the mechanisation of the British Army and transform the way in which troops were supplied.

This was how Bill described the origins of his corps in a speech for Salute the Soldier Week in 1944:

> My Corps, the Royal Army Ordnance Corps, is one of the oldest Corps in the Army, as in bye-gone days it was responsible for supplying the Army with bows and arrows and armour for the men at Arms. In fact, I believe in the early stages of our history we planted the yew forests, from which the bows were made.[11]

At the time of the invasion by William the Conqueror, it is probable that the Roman tower on the Thames (now the Tower of London) housed the army's arms. For most of its history the organisation that controlled the arms came under the leadership of the Master General of Ordnance. This was one of the great offices of state, once held by the Duke of Wellington. It was a powerful office: he who holds the key to the armour has power both to support the Crown and to oppose it. It seems that it was also a profitable office and so, inevitably, the time came for Parliament to rein it in.[12]

The story that followed appears to be one of duplication and inefficiency. The key issue was that the ordnance function was to be kept separate from the army itself. There were periods when successful patterns of working emerged, but it seemed that, once a crisis passed, lessons were forgotten. The South African War and its aftermath led at least to a structure for ordnance with an AOC under the Quartermaster General (QMG), but with a separate Army Ordnance Department (AOD) under the Master General of Ordnance still responsible for production and purchasing. In logistics terms, the AOC was still separate from transport, which fell within the remit of the Army Service Corps, which also fed the troops – hardly an example of efficiency, although at least both corps came within the QMG's department.[13]

War memorial at COD Chilwell.

The Great War saw an expansion in the AOC, from thirty officers and 1,360 men in 1914 to 800 officers and 38,000 men in 1918. The war, like all wars, was a learning experience, but it was largely a static war notwithstanding the introduction of the tank. Ordnance bases were formed well behind the front with ammunition and ordnance stores brought forward by rail. AOC personnel ran the supply depots behind the scenes but also the line of supply and the field depots which provided divisions with what they needed in order to fight. The officers and men had clearly conducted themselves with distinction since, after the war, General Sir Travers Clarke, QMG for France, had this to say about the corps: 'Ordnance was the ever-present help of the British soldier in an ordeal of unexampled severity.' The Army Ordnance Corps was rewarded in 1918 by the addition of the word 'Royal' to its name.[14]

1920 – WOOLWICH, ENGLAND

In spite of the great contribution the corps made in the Great War and perhaps because of its history, corps officers were not eligible for Staff College alongside officers in other regiments. Accordingly, the newly named RAOC took the initiative of introducing a course for its own officers. The first such course took place in 1920 at Red Barracks, Woolwich, the old home of the RAOC. Both Bill and Dickie attended and Bill described Dickie as the 'life and soul'. This was really where their friendship began.

The course results are still in the corps archive[15] and show Bill passing out second to Alfred Goldstein, who would go on to command the corps in Malta during the siege and then COD (Central Ordnance Depot) Greenford, which was to play such a big role on D-Day. Other names on that list also reappear in the story: Charles de Wolff, who would command the massive armaments depot at Donnington in Shropshire; G.A. Palmer, who would take on the setting up of Bicester, the key depot that would supply D-Day; C. Cansdale, who would head up ordnance in the British Army of the Rhine; and W.E.C. Pickthall, who would become Director of Ordnance Services (DOS) for the 1st Army in North Africa. In subsequent years other names appear: Brigadier Whitaker, who would succeed Bill at Chilwell and go on to control provisioning in the Middle East; Brigadier Denninston and Colonel Cutforth, who would command ordnance within the 21st Army Group on D-Day; and 'Digger' Reynolds, also a Chilwell pioneer, who was part of the corps' representation in Washington that played such a key role in the supply chain.

Herbert Ellis, of *Autocar* magazine on 16 June 1944,[16] reported an invasion-eve visit to an RAOC Vehicle Reserve Depot (VRD) where transport was massed for the assault on France. He began, though, with a piece of serendipitous history also connected with Woolwich but referring to Chilwell:

One afternoon in 1921, a number of Mark IV and Mark V tanks, which a few years previously had rumbled over the battlefields of Flanders, were delivered at Woolwich Arsenal, the peacetime depot of the Royal Army Ordnance Corps. These tanks were obsolete and clumsy, yet their arrival at Woolwich represented a milestone in the history of the RAOC. It marked the point at which the Corps, not previously concerned with the supply of motor vehicles to the Army, began to set up which is now the greatest distributive system the motor trade of Europe has ever seen or is likely to see.

The *London Evening News* of 2 April 1941[17] described ordnance services in the context of 'Q', the Quartermaster General to the forces who was responsible for all manner of supplies and stores. It was the 'Quartermaster's Stores' of the old song. The *Evening News* told how 'Q' 'sees to Tommy's every need', just like the 'Q' much loved of James Bond. The 'Q' activity ranged from the weekly cost of feeding the army abroad (about £1.5 million, including some 925,000 loaves of bread daily) and the weekly petrol bill at home and overseas of £290,000. Then came the three branches of ordnance services, the RAOC itself: clothing, equipment and accommodation stores; weapons, radio and mechanical transport; and engineering & maintenance.

The increased emphasis on mechanical and technical stores changed the nickname of the RAOC to the 'Rag and Oil Company' and the corps became one of skilled tradesmen.

1934 – CATTERICK, ENGLAND

Back at Catterick, Bill would have contemplated the task ahead. In his mind there were perhaps two competing feelings, the first must have been of satisfaction. One memory of that first ordnance officers' course was of Bill being derided by the others for knowing so little maths. This was a simple result of leaving school at 15. The army, though, like the rest of society, was obsessed with status and background. Promotion was based simply on seniority. In Bill's papers there is a schedule with the names of fellow officers set in order so that he could work out when his time would come. For much of the army, this didn't change until 1944 when Field Marshal Montgomery replaced many long-serving officers with younger men of greater ability.[18] Yet Bill, at age 43, had been given the most crucial job in the whole of Army Ordnance. Maybe the powers that be didn't realise just how vital it was, but Major General Basil Hill, then head of the RAOC, clearly did. Later, Bill spoke of the support he received from Hill but also from Major General Lionel Hoare, the principal ordnance officer in charge of Woolwich:

> They backed me through thick and thin and when I sometimes had to perhaps break the rules, force the pace, go right over their heads to Finance Branches at the War Office and Treasury, they never criticised me for this because they knew I was doing it for the good of Chilwell and the Army. They pulled my leg of course, quite a lot, but I want you to realise that without the backing of these magnificent men, particularly Lionel Hoare, who was constantly visiting me, I could never have achieved so much in so short a time.[19]

The second feeling was probably of terror; here was a project as monumental as it was crucial and it was down to him. The Chilwell site was almost exactly one square mile, an irony for Bill, since as boy he had dreamed of working in the other more famous square mile of the City of London. The experience of war had changed that. Four years in the trenches of Flanders and the experience of making the line of supply actually work or, more probably, a realisation of just how difficult it was to supply an army in the heat of battle, and also the potential of what was possible, had given him the vision of a truly mobile army. In the fullness of time this square mile would be filled by vehicles of all types, repair shops and neatly stacked spare parts, but on a scale that would make the motor manufacturers' own depots look childlike.

There were already builders on-site with a maintenance brief and so it made sense to walk round with them. Bill would have driven down the A1 and then across to Nottingham to meet Frank Perks of the Long Eaton builders, F. Perks & Son, whom he already knew well from Catterick. They had clearly developed a sound working relationship and friendship, since Frank would refer to Bill as 'that mad b**** Bill Williams'.

Frank was a small man of great energy. They made their way through the bramble-covered rail tracks, massive sheds with gaping holes in their roofs and then underground to Viscount Chetwynd's pride and joy, the subterranean chamber formerly used for ammunition storage, perfect to shelter thousands of employees when the German bombers arrived. All this was meant to be

secret but, as is so often the case, the local press, the *Long Eaton Advertiser*, sensed what was going on:

> Dame Rumour has a wagging tongue and there are many tall stories told relative to the Chilwell Depot. It is not our job to nail unfounded rumours, but it is quite true that Messrs. F. Perks & Son have staff busily employed at the Depot – on routine maintenance they say. Various instructions issued indicate that in the near future there may be another unit stationed at the Depot, but like many Government schemes 'everything is in the air' at the moment.[20]

1935 – CHILWELL, ENGLAND

Bill took up his post in March 1935 and put together a small team in Farnborough[21] where the rest of the corps' existing vehicles were kept. In the team was Sub-Conductor Dick Hunt[22] who would, as an officer, become Bill's eyes and ears. The rank of sub-conductor was unique to the corps and was equivalent to sergeant major. There was a long tradition of men from this rank receiving commissions, reflecting the value that was attached to experience. Alongside Hunt there were soldiers and civilians each chosen by Bill for their particular skill. Others in the Farnborough team were Digger Reynolds and Basil Cox, who would take command of the huge depot at Tel el-Kebir in Egypt and then Didcot, with its massive volume of general stores.

The money set aside by the Treasury for the new depot – £22,000[23] – was laughable and that was an early task. It took endless argument, hours spent waiting outside offices in Whitehall and diplomacy on a grand scale. Bill made a point of getting to know the junior civil servant who actually looked after the file and then making a fuss of him. It was pointless going to his superior; far more effective to get the bright young man onside to tailor the argument.

Steadily the £22,000 grew. Sappers came on-site alongside the Perks men and the site was cleared of rubbish. New rail tracks were laid and a massive 9-acre building for stores was constructed. Much midnight oil was burnt trying to work out how much space would be needed for spare parts; there was just nothing to go on. As areas of the site were restored the existing vehicles moved in.

Bill visited the Royal Army Service Corps (RASC) vehicle depot at Feltham; the old ordnance depot at Weedon with its stores of small arms; Didcot with its general stores, and, of course, Woolwich with its arsenal of armaments and technical stores. But all of that had been used for yesterday's battles; Chilwell needed something entirely new. This war was going to be about more than guns; it was about a large range of vehicles demanding a range of spare parts running into tens of thousands. Had he a crystal ball, he might have seen an Amazon distribution warehouse. In fact, what they created was the blueprint from which all modern logistics stem. It was the largest motor distribution business in the world.

His relationship with Jaguar prompted him to write to its managing director, Sir William Lyons, but also to the leaders of the other major motor companies, asking to 'pick their brains'. How were those letters received? With shock; the army, which knows how to do everything, asking for help? Shock, however, was followed by a warm willingness to help.

A warm response came from William Rootes. The Rootes Group disappeared in the 1960s, although its marks of Humber, Hillman and Sunbeam continued a little longer as part of Chrysler and then Peugeot. In the 1930s Rootes, in many ways, led the British motor industry. William Rootes was chairman of the Society of Motor Manufacturers & Traders. His company was very profitable and he lived on an estate in Berkshire where he rubbed shoulders with the great and the good.[24] I am sure it wouldn't be totally unfair to say that he saw benefit in being public spirited, in offering his expertise. But he offered it well beyond what was expedient. He invited Bill down to the Humber works at Coventry where he could see at first hand the operation of a production line.

There were other trips too, to Dagenham and Ford, Vauxhall at Luton, Austin, Morris and Wolseley, and, of course, his beloved Jaguar. It wouldn't just be cars, key components were also required and so trips were made to Fort Dunlop, Lucas and Triplex. Trucks would play a huge part and so visits to AEC and Commer ensued.[25] These trips were reciprocated, with senior motor industry men visiting Chilwell: Sir Peter Bennett and Bob Lillico of Lucas, Harold Kenwood of Dunlop and Sir Patrick Hennessy, Sir Roland Smith and Stanford Cooper of Ford.[26] One result of these visits was the building of a comradeship between the Chilwell officers and the civilian firms who would supply them, which would last for the duration of the war and beyond.

Another highly influential visitor was Lord Nuffield, who had been to see Chilwell and had told the War Minister, Mr Hore Belisha, about all that was happening. So when, in the summer of 1939, the question of an appointment as Deputy Director of Ordnance Services (MT) came up, the War Minister asked, 'Why not Williams at Chilwell?'[27]

Motor industry expertise was a prerequisite, but only if a system could be found to enable stock to be located quickly and monitored effectively. It would be pointless having vehicles and all the necessary spares if the men

Visidex system at work at COD Chilwell.

had to scrape round to find them. The big retail stores would help with this, and so more letters and trips to Marks & Spencer, Woolworths and Harrods ensued. Bill's friendly civil servant also suggested that the Metropolitan Police had a good system. Everything was up for grabs.

The choice that Bill made was controversial, since it ignored the mechanical and electronic systems that were already emerging. He decided to use Visidex, a manual card system that reduced duplication and could be used both in depots and in the field; a factor that would prove decisive.

1938 – CHILWELL, ENGLAND

Chilwell marked a dramatic transition from the army of old to something entirely new. Mr B.H. Shepherd was one of 1,300 civilians who worked there in 1938 and he recalled the day when the Royal Artillery stabled their horses for the last time:

The Chestnut Troop RA reported to the Vehicle Kit Store in smart riding breeches and with spurs a-jingling on their boots, whips under left arm, chin straps in position with service cap on head. At a command from the Battery Sergeant-Major they marched in file, halted at the Kit Store, stood at ease and received the keys to the new mechanical horses and a maintenance kit also. Standing outside the store were olive green 4-wheeled drive Quad-Ant Tractors made by Guy Motors, for towing guns and limber – mechanisation had arrived for them. The RA was now on wheels and bound for Salisbury Plain; in future the cost for the loss of any item of kit would be deductible from the Gunner's pay![28]

The Chilwell project had taken three years and by 26 April 1938 it was ready to be revealed to the public. A visit was arranged for the press. It was still shrouded in secrecy; the depot had to be referred to as 'somewhere in the Midlands' and Bill could not be named. Cuttings from that visit add more flavour:[29]

Bedford OXC radio vehicle. (© Vauxhall Heritage Archive)

THE TIMES
KEEPING THE ARMY MOBILE

The mechanisation of the Army has thrown a heavy responsibility on the Royal Army Ordnance Corps, the duties of which include the purchase, supply, and maintenance of motor vehicles in addition to the supplying of arms and ammunition …

Every modern development has been embodied in the depot. There is one shed enclosing eleven acres under its roof and another covering nine designed to house the multiplicity of material required. The variety of the material is impressive. Heavy gun tractors, tractors for anti-aircraft equipment, breakdown lorries, office vans, wireless carriers, pontoon carrying lorries and the innumerable small vehicles used by the infantry.

The system of maintenance for motor vehicles was demonstrated yesterday. Units are provided with light aid detachments, rather like the small veterinary units which were allotted to mounted units in the old days, and in addition the RAOC has established well equipped workshops in every military centre to carry out the bigger repairs.

THE DAILY TELEGRAPH
ARMY TRANSPORT READY

'If the Field Army were mobilised tomorrow, all the units, without exception, could have their transport vehicles immediately raised from a peace to a war footing.'

Mobile repair workshop. (RLC Museum)

Bill Williams' quoted remark above may well have returned to haunt him after Dunkirk. In 1938, though, the press were impressed. Again, from the *Daily Telegraph*:

> Every detail has been worked out ready to equip base depots and field parks in any part of the world. As regards trained personnel, the depot is staffed with soldiers and ex-soldiers. Should the soldiers proceed overseas on mobilisation to form base depots, arrangements are made to ensure that there are sufficient civilian 'key' men left behind to carry on the 'load' at the Home Army Ordnance Depot.

The *Press Association* opted for something more prosaic:

MILES OF MOTOR VEHICLES: MILLIONS OF SPARE PARTS

> Napoleon had an idea that an army marches on its stomach, but, if he could have joined a party of pressmen today who paid a visit to a certain army mechanisation depot in the Midlands, he would probably have agreed that nowadays the army marches on wheels.
>
> There are not only miles of tractors, tanks and every type of motor vehicle, but there are sheds, hundreds of yards long, containing no fewer than 75,000 different kinds of spare parts to keep these vehicles efficient and up to date. It is no exaggeration to say that in all there are more than ten million spare parts carefully graded and packed ready for dispatch at any moment.

The *Daily Express* highlighted the role of women, but also the vehicles and their drivers. It seems that it was the *Express* which spilled the beans on the final cost of some £1 million. The *Daily Herald* rejoiced in the absence of 'red tape'. They also told of a mobile office with its own telephone exchange, duplicators and map room all contained within a truck.

The *Yorkshire Post* reported that the depot was staffed by forty officers, 300 soldiers and 1,300 civilians, adding that the number of soldiers would shortly be increased to 1,000. Almost as an aside they wrote that several hundred young women were employed, mostly as clerical staff. The role of women would become increasingly important as the war progressed. The *Post* did add some flavour by disclosing the destination of some of the vehicles they saw:

SUPER-EFFICIENT ORGANISATION

> I saw huge sand-coloured wireless vehicles ready for bodily shipment to the East. Recently a Division en route for Palestine was provided with complete mechanical transport and equipment in three days; an illustration of the efficiency of the centre – and the importance of and necessity for that efficiency.

The amount of press interest the story generated could well indicate the hunger the public had for news about rearmament. The visit was clearly well organised and invitations were issued to all the right people, and the great Richard Dimbleby recorded a piece for the BBC. Technical journals such as *The Engineer* homed in on detail:

ARMY MECHANISATION

> A main component store adjoins a railway siding and an access road served by overhead electric cranes … in addition to the usual equipment for a workshop of this kind, it had a machine shop equipped with a good selection of modern machines, a blacksmiths shop, an electrical vetting and repair section, paint spraying booths, a sheet metal working section and a welding department.

Engine repair workshop at COD Chilwell.

Trimmers' workshop at COD Chilwell.

Motorcycle repairs at COD Chilwell.

Joiners' and carpenters' workshop at COD Chilwell.

Workshop lifting gear at COD Chilwell.

Battery storage at COD Chilwell.

Blacksmiths' workshop at COD Chilwell.

Assembly workshop at COD Chilwell.

The *Manchester Guardian* allowed itself a little poetic licence:

HUGE CENTRAL DEPOT FOR MECHANISED REARMAMENT

Two years ago the British Army had about 4,000 motor-vehicles. Today it is 22,500.

'If I had such splendid men,' said Hyder Ali two centuries ago, speaking of the British Soldier, 'I would take greater care of them than you do. They should never march on foot but be carried in palanquins on men's shoulders, and then, when we got near the enemy, they should get out fresh and rested, and I would let them loose as we slip the cheetahs in hunting deer.' It would seem that Hyder Ali's suggestion is coming into its own after two centuries.

A day at this centre is a dizzy experience. Everything runs smoothly and quietly at inspection benches, in the component stores department, where parts are in special steel racking, indexed like a good library and not unlike one in appearance, for the department has to deal with about 500 requisitions a day; at the service station, with its two powerful lifts; and in the department where war reserves of engines, back axles, and similar large units are packed specially to stand rough handling in the field and stacked high to get the maximum number of cases on the minimum of storage space.

The office is about as big as Albert Square, Manchester, and its different departments and clerks are fed with their work by a moving belt which passes down the middle. Some 3,500 transactions a day pass through it.

It may have been all the publicity, but one young soldier took it upon himself to try to destroy what had been created. Early on Wednesday, 10 May 1939, residents of Chilwell, Beeston, Long Eaton and places for miles around watched as a blaze took hold of the Chilwell tyre store. The store was rebuilt and Bill later reflected that the fire had been a blessing in disguise since the replacement store was designed specifically for tyres, something that would reap benefits over the coming years.

Absolutely key to Chilwell, but more so to the corps as whole, would be the right men. There were good soldiers whom Bill knew from Italy, the Rhine and Catterick, and, of course, others. But it was more than soldiers; Chilwell, and again the corps as whole, was more than an army depot, it was a business, one of the 'biggest businesses in the world'. Bill set out the task as he saw it in a letter dated February 1939:[30]

Office conveyor at COD Chilwell.

MT component store, COD Chilwell.

Right: 30cwt stacker, COD Chilwell.

Far right: Electric elevator for tyres at COD Chilwell.

Right: Lister truck at COD Chilwell.

The RAOC will require in war a large number of temporary officers with sound training in business organisation. There is no doubt that, with the vast expansion which will take place, the efficiency of the Ordnance Services will largely depend on the standard and experience of these new officers.

The production staff of the manufacturers will of course be employed, in most cases, on munition production, but the general organising, distributing and sales staffs will be largely redundant in war, and it is in this field that we shall find some of the best business executives in the country.

This is the material required for the RAOC, men with drive, imagination, initiative and a sound training in business organisation with a possible technical background.

The Munich crisis in September 1938 had nudged a reluctant British Government a step closer to a serious preparation for war. In the case of the RAOC this manifested itself in the opening of a register called the Army Officers Emergency Reserve, with the help of the motor industry. William Rootes stepped forward to head up the initiative and gathered the names of many talented men in the motor industry who would later play an important part in the transformation of the RAOC. In a speech in March 1942, Bill looked back over this period of vital activity:

Throughout the hectic summer of 1939 we were completing our arrangements to recruit for the RAOC the businessmen who would have to run it in wartime. I wrote to the Trade Associations, to the great commercial undertakings of this country, to the motor manufacturers, to Dunlops, to Marks and Spencers, to Woolworths, to Harrods, and so on, asking for their best men. I wrote in particular to the firms which paid the biggest salaries because they are the firms which had the best brains. We wanted those brains in the RAOC.

Two great firms raised complete companies of specially selected men, and I cannot tell you the relief it was to have men of this type, all of whom held good jobs in civil life by virtue of energy and drive, and the result is that today we have an organisation of which we are proud.

And, we recruited many hundreds of skilled business executives – men who were fully alive to the situation, who were keen and eager to learn, and who brought with them a great wealth of experience and knowledge.

Bill later recorded that he had sent out 2,000 letters to businesses and the first response had been a phone call from Simon Marks of Marks & Spencer. The two men met that evening and explored the possibilities. After the war, Bill wrote to Simon, saying of the M&S men:[31]

They served in all parts of the world where British troops were engaged, and also provided an important part of my staff in America who were engaged in intricate and delicate negotiations with the American Army and Manufacturers connected with the supply of vast quantities of war material which we received under lend-lease.

The Commercial Vehicle Users' Journal of October 1944[32] carried an article entitled, 'Mechanising the British Army – The Romantic Story of Chilwell – and the part played by the Motor Industry in converting a Derelict Factory into a Gigantic Mechanical transport Depot'. At the end it lists those RAOC officers connected with the motor trade. In all, 500 men from the motor industry played significant roles in the RAOC. A good number feature by name in this story: Colonel Dan Warren came from SS Cars; Colonel Robinson was Chief Ordnance Officer (COO) at COD Derby and converted Feltham into a COD; and Colonel Hiam was COO Old Dalby and then COO of 15 AOD (Advance Ordnance Depot) in Antwerp both came from Dunlop. Colonel Sewell, who took over COD Feltham, came from Tecalamit; Colonel Browne, who went out to India to set up 206 IBOD, was from Morris Motors; Colonel McCausland, who was an ever-present source of inspiration at Chilwell, came from Provincial & Suburban Garages Ltd; J.W. Mackillop from Jackson Garages, Aberdeen, later commanded the Tanks & Vehicles Organisation, and Colonel Johnson-Davis, who was the first commander at COD Greenford, was from the Motor Trade Association.

The invasion of Czechoslovakia provoked Chamberlain into announcing a second initiative that would prove vital, the call-up of men aged between 20 and 21 for six months' training. Some 3,900 joined the RAOC. In May 1939 the RAOC opened a training establishment for apprentice mechanics and tradesmen and so put in place a formal programme of training in the skills that would be needed. In his March 1942 speech Bill also referred to this aspect:

We tackled the Other Ranks' problem on exactly the same lines. I wrote thousands of personal letters to the heads of the great firms throughout the country setting out a picture of the problems with which we were faced, the intricate types of stores with which we have to deal and the classes and types of men required to carry out the work.

The big business undertakings and the trade associations of this country, provided me with many thousands of volunteer recruits who possessed the necessary background and experience or who had the right type of brain and business training to enable them to rapidly assimilate the enormous problems with which we were faced. Incidentally the vast majority of our officers today, at any rate the junior ones, were commissioned from the ranks of these younger recruits after a probationary and training period.

In response to this, the Society of Motor Manufacturers & Traders in Birmingham formed their own Territorial unit, with many from Dunlop. This unit eventually became 5 Ordnance Field Park and 14 Field Workshop, which was to reach Berlin in 1945.

Albert Griffiths[33] was employed as a motor mechanic at a firm called Prestage, the Midland distributor of Vauxhall cars and Bedford trucks. He and a number of fellow workmates joined the unit, which was commanded by their managing director, Lieutenant Colonel (TA) Walter Prestage.

Other parts of the motor industry were approached, with success measured by the standing joke at Chilwell about the 'Lucas Light Infantry' and 'Rootes Rifles'.[34]

Edward Sieff, of Marks & Spencer, sent this letter to his staff:

This will provide our employees who have already registered or are about to register for military service, with an opportunity of serving in HM Forces with their own colleagues, and making full use of the experience which they have gained with the company.[35]

The result was a company made up entirely of M&S men.

These initiatives, taken together, meant that the RAOC would not be totally unprepared for war when the time came, or, as Bill put it:

The results have been electrifying. The experiment has been a complete success. These men have introduced new methods and new ideas into the RAOC. They have made it possible for us to bear the tremendous burden of equipping the British Army, of equipping our allies, of supplying fighting fronts throughout the world and of keeping Lord Beaverbrook's promise of aid to Russia.

The challenge of war tested this assertion to breaking point.

THE BRITISH EXPEDITIONARY FORCE

The time for testing came at 11 a.m. on Sunday, 3 September 1939, when war was declared. Bill Williams, now Deputy Director of Ordnance Services (MT) at the War Office, went to Chilwell that morning to lead a group of senior serving officers meeting, possibly for the first time, the newly called up members of the Army Officers Emergency Reserve. These latter included 'Reddy' Readman, who would take over as COO at Chilwell; Bob Hiam, who would command the depot at Old Dalby; Robby Robinson, who would command the depot at Sinfin Lane, Derby; and Dan Warren, who would take a lead role in 'scaling', the dark art of estimating the quantity of spare parts needed to maintain vehicles in battle order.

Also on that Sunday in Birmingham the executives of the Nuffield Motor Company met to put into action the plans they had prepared for war.[1] Through the various parts of the Nuffield Group it would, over the next five years, contribute aircraft and weapon production in addition to a great many vehicles. The remainder of the big five motor companies had been working with the government on preparations for war, mainly the manufacture of aircraft. On that Sunday, though, the car plants themselves were placed on a war footing. The men who arrived for work the following day would be instructed to complete those cars already started, but then to ready the shop floor for war production. In many cases the contracts were slow in coming and the companies had to keep their workforces occupied one way or another; some had to be laid off. The motor industry, because it was set up to manufacture on a production line largely with metal, and because it had a broad range of other skilled men, would be more than busy for the next five

or six years. The 1939 Motor Show was cancelled and very few domestic cars would be produced until the war ended.[2]

For the 2 million or so car owners then in Britain, the sunshine of that first Sunday in September would bring them out for possibly the last recreational trip for some years. Many better off British motorists converged on the Channel ports in the hope of getting home from what could be their last continental holiday. Many did, but some left their much loved tourers behind.[3]

Elsewhere, plans were in hand for mass evacuation from urban areas. Gas masks had been issued and a blackout imposed. Britain was at war. Mobilisation had been ordered on Friday, 1 September and, at the RAOC's new headquarters at Hilsea near Portsmouth, it took the corps by surprise simply because of the sheer numbers (6,000) who had volunteered and been allocated for ordnance work.

This needs to be set in context. At the point when the nation went to war, the total strength of the whole RAOC at home and abroad was 727 officers and 5,292 soldiers. Indeed, the War Office estimate of the likely number of recruits had been only a misleadingly precise 237 men. The huge influx initially overwhelmed the small recruitment team and it also necessitated the taking over of every school building in north Portsmouth and Cosham. The NAAFI was quite unable to cope; it was only the absence of rationing and the use of local purchasing that saved the day. At Hilsea there was neither enough space, nor uniforms, nor equipment. To compound the problem, the corps was responsible for supplying not only itself but the army as a whole. In time, things began to settle, but it was very much 'make-do and mend'.[4]

Hillsea Barracks, RAOC HQ.

SOME OF THE PEOPLE

The story of the mechanisation of the army could be told just with figures and statistics, and there will be room for some of these. However, the story is far more about people: men and women, not necessarily attracted by soldiering but called up and finding a crucial role for themselves and their skills in this enormous machine.

James Child[5] was a production engineer at Rootes, Coventry, who signed up for the Territorials and had been assigned to searchlight duties in Coventry. He was later given a commission and sent on a four-month gun course, an expertise he would put to good use in the desert.

On joining up, Albert Griffiths[6] and the others in the Prestage unit formed in Birmingham earlier in the year, found themselves sleeping on beds with no mattresses on the metal springs and no meal available on the evening of their arrival. Following initial training, Albert was also sent off on an armament artificers course at Chilwell, while the remainder of the unit left for France and later suffered heavy casualties, including the commanding officer (CO).

James Welford[7] was an apprentice at the Witton works of GEC and, with a number of others, enlisted in the Territorials at Fort Dunlop in Birmingham. On the declaration of war they became His Majesty's 14th Army Field Workshop of the Royal Army Ordnance Corps and in January 1940 sailed to Cherbourg.

Wilfred Beeson[8] had a small motor mechanics business in Chiswick, but on 3 September presented himself at the recruitment centre in North Acton. He was sent down to Hilsea with some 1,000 other volunteers. His skills as a mechanic were identified and he was sent out to France within five days of joining up. He was part of the 8th Army Field Workshop.

Private John Frost[9] was already a Territorial with a searchlight regiment. He was a tidy man, probably happiest at a desk or with his hobby of collecting newspapers. A number of companies (Unilever, in John's case) had encouraged employees to join Territorial units and emphasis had been given to anti-aircraft protection. John remembered peacetime activity as relatively gentle, and in particular being called out at the end of August and then being sent home since 'nothing was ready'. He returned on the Saturday and he recalled the chill as an officer read the Articles of War. The informality of peace had gone and there they were, shut in with a guard on the gate. John would later play a number of roles in the RAOC.

Alwyn Ward[10] also joined the Territorials in the summer of 1939 and, on being mobilised on the declaration of war, became a fitter in the RAOC. He recalls having to sleep on floorboards in a church hall and then undergoing drill and fitness training, before being sent to St Pol as part of the 9th Army Field Workshop in January 1940. He was later selected to join the newly formed Royal Electrical & Mechanical Engineers (REME) and became an armament artificer with the rank of armament staff sergeant, before joining the invasion of North Africa.

Corn merchant Douglas Hanson[11] joined the Territorials in March 1939. On mobilisation he was sent out to the Base Ordnance Depot at Nantes. He would later be caught up in the surrender of Singapore.

Another Rootes man, Douglas Postlethwaite,[12] was working for Humber Cars and enlisted at Coventry a little later, in December 1939. He was sent on a fitter's course at Standard Cars near Shepherds Bush before being sent out to convoy duty in France. He would later join the field workshop of the 21st Tank Brigade and serve in North Africa.

The experience of Wally Harris[13] was a little different. He was a motor mechanic and had enrolled as a Territorial at the Chelsea Barracks. On mobilisation he was called up to join the 1st London Division Ordnance Workshop at a brand new building in Mill Hill. It was so new it had no equipment, not even work benches. He was billeted at Hendon Golf Club and slept in the changing rooms. There was one rifle between five men and the only vehicles were very old. His was a Thorneycroft lorry with an open cab, solid tyres and a crash gearbox. The 1st London became the 56th Black Cats and the ordnance men were divided up into Light Aid Detachments (LADs) of twelve men; his was attached to the 168 London Infantry Brigade. The LAD was made up of men with skills ranging from electrician and storeman to mechanic. As he put it, it was the AA or RAC for army vehicles, only they weren't obviously army vehicles at all, being butchers' vans and delivery lorries all in their original colours. He remembered the feeling of embarrassment when driving these vehicles in convoy. He remembered, too, that they were very short of equipment; he resorted to bringing his own tools from home. His unit remained in London and the south-east and he recalled being very fed up at seeing no action.

A MECHANISED ARMY?

The main focus of the mobilisation, though, was on equipping the BEF. On 11 September the BEF crossed the Channel and began to dig in on the Belgian border. The report on the performance of the RAOC in the BEF[14] provides detail that paints a picture of the scale of what had been prepared over the summer months. By 27 September, the following had been shipped to France: 152,031 army personnel; 9,392 air force personnel; 21,424 army vehicles; 2,470 air force vehicles; 36,000 tons of ammunition; 25,000 tons of motor spirit and 60,000 tons of frozen meat. The numbers hide the gremlins of organisation, such as troops sailing with the promise that their equipment would be 'waiting for them on the other side' (it seldom was), troops and their equipment being shipped to different ports and a chronic shortage of accommodation stores.

The report began with these words: 'The British Army which crossed to France in 1939 differed from other armies at that time in being fully mechanised.' The report continued, 'The Army was however better equipped on paper than in practice.'[15] Subsequent histories of the period point to the army being ill-equipped. It was said that 'transport consisted of vans and lorries from post offices, butchers and other commercial companies, painted khaki and often in bad repair'.[16] There was some truth in this since, certainly, vehicles had been commandeered. Nevertheless, it was also the case that the War office had commissioned the design and production of a range of army lorries. For example, Vauxhall began the war with the delivery of many

Vehicle convoy ready to depart COD Chilwell, 1939.

thousands of Bedford trucks. In time, a number of variations on the basic model were produced including an all-wheel-drive that would revert to a single-axle drive in normal road conditions.[17] Hogg and Weeks[18] suggest that of 85,000 vehicles in September 1939, 21,500 were motorcycles and 26,000 trucks and other vehicles that had been impressed; this leaves a good number that were purpose built.

The *Commercial Vehicles Users' Journal* of October 1944,[19] which had set out the list of those motor men who had joined the RAOC, also offered a description of the vehicles:

Many and varied were the types produced; one firm alone got out a series of prototypes numbering some two dozen in all and including 6-wheelers, 8-wheelers, half-tracks and armoured cars and although much of the research was unprofitable, it at any rate led to there being some suitable types ready when war broke out. Nevertheless, most of the vehicles the BEF were able to take with them to France in 1939 were very largely adaptions of civilian models except for a few tracked vehicles of the Bren gun carrier nature. Most of the original vehicles were of course lost in the evacuation from Dunkirk. By that time, real progress was being made

Austin 7 and Morris 8 store, COD Chilwell.

Heavy vehicles ready for the BEF, COD Chilwell.

Motorcycle store, COD Chilwell.

in the design and production of vehicles capable of doing a war job and Brigadier Williams facilitated visits to France on the part of manufactures during the winter of 1939/40.

The army had thus been provided with a staggering array of different vehicles. All the manufacturers took on the task of training those RAOC (later REME) engineers whose job it would be to maintain them. In time, a good number of civilian motor engineers joined up as officers to undertake the training role in-house. Alongside training there was also the provision of detailed vehicle handbooks. For example, on the outbreak of war many Bedford trucks were taken over from their owners for army purposes. Few of these came with the relevant handbook and so these had to be supplied. For Vauxhall, a variation on the theme appeared in the form of a book called simply *For B.E.s*. It seems that the manufacturers became sick and tired of soldiers making the same mistakes time and again. The book, illustrated by Douglas of *Punch*, became famous worldwide. It was translated into several languages and much was reproduced verbatim by the Americans in an instruction book dealing with armoured vehicles.

Troop carrier in use by BEF. (RLC Museum)

In spite of all of this, the well-rehearsed reluctance of the government to rearm meant that, very simply, not enough army equipment had been manufactured, not least with the emphasis being placed on aircraft production. Production was at nothing like a warlike tempo, with the result that there was little, if anything, in reserve. The report on the BEF[20] offers some figures which give a sense of the scale of the shortfall:

At the beginning of December 1939 there were only 70 infantry tanks out of a requirement of 204 and it was expected that by the end of February 1940 there would only be 130 out of a requirement of 461. Other serious deficiencies were in anti-tank guns, light anti-aircraft guns, vehicles and signals stores … modern artillery was also scarce and the Army had to go into battle with obsolete guns such as the 4.5 inch howitzer of 1914–18 vintage.

Yet it wasn't only a matter of numbers; it was the very fact that for the first time an army had been fully mechanised, and inevitably there would be many lessons to learn.

BRITISH MOTOR INDUSTRY

Mechanisation was, as much as anything, a determining factor in the Second World War. At Chilwell, Bill Williams had approached industry for advice and help; the input of industry was very much wider than that. One British commercial organisation that had a strong influence on the mechanisation of the British Army was the Rootes Group. Under the leadership of the highly entrepreneurial Billy, later Lord Rootes, in the 1920s the company became the world's largest car and truck distributor with the wonderful slogan 'cars packed, shipped and delivered to all parts of the world'.[21] The story of the growth of this company is relevant.

Having found that they had generated more demand for motor cars than could be fulfilled from existing sources, the Rootes brothers entered the field of manufacturing with the purchase of the ailing Humber, Hillman and Commer companies in 1928. They then introduced American methods of production and promoted the design of cars for the 1930s.

Billy Rootes was quoted as saying, 'I don't mind what I sell, provided it is British'.[22] When the storm clouds began to gather in 1936, this attitude turned itself into a fierce patriotism. Billy was on a tour of the Far East with his son, Geoffrey, when in Singapore he received a telegram inviting him to become chairman of a committee the government was forming with the task of setting up a shadow industry to manufacture aircraft at 'new and exciting' factories in Britain. He immediately cabled back his acceptance, and from then on the Rootes Group was at the forefront of the government's scheme to organise the volume production of airframes and aircraft.[23]

In May 1937, Billy and his brother Reggie, the 'steadying hand of the group',[24] visited Speke near Liverpool where they were planning the first of the shadow factories for the production of bombers. The factory was designed to enable raw materials to be brought in at one end and for completed aircraft to come out at the other:

A special feature was the electrically operated overhead railway, located high up in the roof of the main assembly shop and erecting hall, which allowed large aeroplane sections and even entire airframes to be transported from one section of the building to another without causing any interference to the work being done in the other areas below.[25]

Although principally a motor vehicle manufacturer, the two Rootes factories produced more than 50,000 aero engines between 1939 and 1945 and repaired a further 20,000 made by other manufacturers.[26] The factory design was to influence the layout of many RAOC depots.

It wasn't only the Rootes Group, other motor manufacturers were approached and were contributing to the war effort in their various ways. A key factor in common was that they were 'metal bashers' and a great deal of the material needed for war was 'bashed metal', from ammunition to aircraft. The factories offered appropriate space and skilled men who were adept at retooling for a whole variety of different jobs. The men had a range of skills: there were carpenters, electricians, men skilled with heavy cloth, as well as blacksmiths and metal fabricators.

The group of motor companies headed by Lord Nuffield, with factories in Birmingham, Coventry and Oxford (Cowley), played many and varied parts. Lord Nuffield was a single-minded, patriotic entrepreneur. He saw the threat from Germany building in the mid-1930s and set up, as an offshoot of the Riley Company, a factory to manufacture aero engines. In spite, or perhaps because, of the fact that this was at his own expense and initiative, the Air Ministry declined to make use of it. Later it became clear very early in the war that the RAF was 'wasting' a great many planes, in the sense that planes crashed and could no longer fly. Nuffield was commissioned to set up a network of Civil Repair Organisations which would collect the crashed aircraft, bring them to repair factories in various parts of the country and, largely by trial and error, put them back into airworthy condition. This massive operation provided vital support in the Battle of Britain.[27] It, like the other major motor companies, manufactured anything from trucks to ammunition and steel helmets.

SKILLS

In January 1940, Billy Rootes was asked by the War Office to go with Bill Williams to visit France and advise on the servicing and maintenance of vehicles for the BEF. 'Many of the vehicles concerned were Humbers, Hillmans and Commers and Billy was keen to organise major unit overhaul and exchange schemes, to speed up heavy repair operations and introduce important economies.'[28] After two months he delivered his report, which found serious shortcomings in the knowledge of motor transport requirements within the army. The RAOC had recruited into officer ranks electrical, civil and mechanical engineers, rather than men who had practical knowledge of motor transport. He therefore recommended that 'experienced men from the motor industry should be identified and given special intensive training in army methods and discipline and be sent to France as soon as possible'.[29] Another area of shortcoming was in the deployment of skilled mechanics, many of whom were spending too much time on fatigues and so not taking full advantage of their particular skills. 'The Army didn't take kindly to all the criticisms, but urgent measures had to be taken to solve the problems and the majority of the recommendations were put into effect.'[30]

It wasn't only the lack of technical expertise, RAOC officers were soldiers too. The massive expansion of the corps had the effect of putting men into the field who had been in the Reserve and so who had limited experience of the practical operation of ordnance in the field. This, combined with the fact that mobilisation had taken away experienced men from the depots, meant that staffing was a challenge – to say the least.

TANKS

British tanks were considered, even by the British, to be inferior to their German counterparts at the beginning of the war, so much so that it was said that numerical superiority of two to one was needed to give the British a chance in direct combat.[31] The reasons behind this situation were quite central to the story of the mechanisation of the army.

The tank had been a British invention, the first examples manufactured by William Foster & Co in Lincoln. The story goes that in 1915 First Lord of the Admiralty Winston Churchill had become horrifically aware of the stalemate of the Western Front and how young men were being slaughtered because, while mankind had invented bullets and shells, it had not yet found an effective defence against them. Thus, time and again the order would come for an advance and, time and again, it would fail with horrific loss of life. What was needed was a machine out of H.G. Wells, a 'landship' protected by steel armour and capable of travelling over trenches, mud and barbed wire. With Churchill's influence it was the navy who made the first prototypes and hence the initial name of Landship.[32] The biggest problem was the sheer weight of armour.

Quite separately, Lieutenant Colonel Swinton, then a war correspondent, had identified the need for 'a power-driven, bullet-proof, armed engine capable of destroying machine guns, of crossing country and trenches, of breaking through entanglements and of climbing earthworks'.[33] Swinton had been told of an earlier invention by Hornsby Agricultural Engineers of Grantham: a tracked vehicle suitable as a cross-country tractor. While the design had won first prize in a 1908 War Office competition, the company had failed to make it a commercial success and so had sold the patented track system to the Holt Tractor Company of California, who had found a strong demand for such a vehicle from their agricultural customers.[34] The Holt system seemed to address the problem of weight.

Contracts were awarded for the production of 100 tracked landships to Foster's, where the naval officer responsible, Walter G. Wilson, had joined William Tritton. The project was, of course, secret and it was made known that the factories were producing motorised water 'tanks' for use in Mesopotamia and the name stuck. Following a period of experimentation, a revised tracked version proved satisfactory and more than 4,000 were produced.

When Churchill returned to office as Minister of Munitions, he resumed oversight of the project and so had a hand in the victory at the Battle of Amiens in August 1918, when 600 British tanks sent terrified Germans into headlong defeat. In time they recovered their cool but, crucially, morale had been broken by this invention in which Churchill had had more than a hand.[35]

Another important element of the story of mechanisation emerging from the Great War was the idea of 'small individual armoured vehicles dashing about the battlefield'.[36] The concept was developed by Carden & Lloyd, in the form of an armoured universal carrier. A good number were sold around the world, and the company was bought by Vickers in

1928. The Mechanised Force test referred to in the previous chapter used these vehicles. The Carden-Lloyd design was to prove influential in later tank design.[37]

Notwithstanding these ground-breaking British inventions, on 7 November 1936 the military correspondent of the *Morning Post* published this report:[38]

> The Tank Brigade is in a sorry plight at the moment. The 12 ton (medium) tank, which is still the armament of that Brigade, is literally falling to pieces. 'Nuts and bolts are strewn about the field when it manoeuvres, and at the end of a battle the casualties give an unintentionally realistic touch to operations.' Until the Tank Brigade has been rearmed it could not take the field without grave risk of disaster.

In 1919 Clough William Ellis, author of the book, *The Tank Corps*, had said, 'Within the period of a generation, a time may come again when we shall have to defend our lives and our liberties. We lead the world in the design

MK I Carrier.

and manufacture of tanks. Let us not abandon that lead in the production of a vital weapon.' The lead had indeed been abandoned for a variety of reasons, as writers from the time explain.

The *Commercial Vehicles Users' Journal* of October 1944 had this to say:

> In those pre-war days when Chilwell was being brought into existence as the MT depot, it was definite policy of those in authority at the War Office to concentrate British production on the light types. The understanding was that the French were producing heavier tanks up to 70 tons. These never materialised and in the event only a fraction of the available British tanks were set against the advancing Panzers, since the very light armour of most of the British tanks made them 'deathtraps'.

Charles Graves, writing in his book on the contribution of the motor industry in the Second World War, *Drive for Freedom*, was more candid when he wrote:

> The War Office, for the 15 years after the end of the First World War and before the rise of Hitler to power did not envisage any wars on the Continent. All that it expected was the possibility of campaigns on the North-West Frontier of India and in the Middle East. Its experts therefore concentrated on small light tanks with 14 mm armour and machine guns capable of coping with hill tribes who would not be equipped with anti-tank guns.[39]

In his book, *World War Two Tanks*, George Forty explains, with perhaps even greater candour and the benefit of hindsight, that the underlying issue was one of under-resource but, almost as important, a lack of clarity of what was needed. It seems that the War Office had stuck to the First World War distinction of light tanks for reconnaissance and scouting missions, medium/cruiser tanks with a mix of speed, firepower and protection to make their presence felt in battle and heavier well-protected tanks to support infantry.

He suggested that the first category was, in effect, a scout car, of which many were manufactured and used in the Second World War and that the other two categories should have been combined, given the necessity for all three attributes of protection, speed and firepower. He observed that no British Second World War tank had the firepower of the British heavy tank of 1916–18, which boasted two 6-pounder guns capable of firing armour piercing (AP), high-explosive (HE) and cased shot, and four machine guns. The champions of First World War tanks, the Old Guard (TOGs), later developed a massive 80-ton machine which was suitable only for First World War style warfare and so never put into production or service.[40]

The practical effect of all this was that in the early 1930s British tank production was almost entirely of light tanks in the hands of Vickers-Armstrongs. Some 550 light Mk VIs went to France with the BEF and all but six were destroyed or left behind.[41]

There were also infantry tanks, the original idea being that they must be protective and effective against infantry; speed was not essential since all it needed was to move with the infantry it supported. Vickers built a series of infantry tanks, called Matildas. A number of Mk II Matildas performed effectively in the Arras counter-attack by the BEF. It also won fans later in the desert until the Germans came on the scene. It was powered by an AEC engine and was 'almost immune to enemy fire except at point blank range'.[42] Once it had ceased its use as a gun tank it continued with valuable roles in mine clearance and as dozers, bridge-layers and flamethrowers.

In the mid-1930s, the Master General of Ordnance, Major General Sir Hugh Elles, had become adamant that Vickers should have competition in tank production and this is where the Nuffield companies entered the picture. They developed medium cruiser tanks with the revolutionary Christie suspension.[43] The story goes that a delegation from the War Office visited Moscow to witness the annual armaments parade and they saw a very basic but very fast tank. On making enquiries they discovered that it was built round a new suspension system, developed by a man called Christie in the United States. The system enabled the tank to go fast, but also relatively smoothly, making it much safer for the driver, who previously would often be knocked out should the tank encounter a sharp undulation in the land it was crossing. Lord Nuffield purchased a Christie tank with his company's own money and then proceeded to develop a new Nuffield tank employing the Christie suspension. The result was the Cruiser. In May 1940 the first few Cruiser tanks arrived in France with 30mm armour, which was more effective but equipped only with 2lb guns that were still no match for the German 6-pounders.

The BEF had also been equipped with half-track armoured cars and the first of the tracked universal carriers, based on the Carden-Lloyd design. Methods of flame cutting and welding armour plate had been developed, with the result that the bodies, or 'hulls', of such vehicles no longer had to be riveted sheets of steel which would spray the occupants with loosened rivets when hit. They were effective and would be developed further as the war progressed.

In short the tank and armoured car provision of the BEF was at best patchy.

VEHICLE SPARE PARTS AND REPAIRS

Motor vehicle spare parts soon became a major headache for a number of reasons. Ordnance stores, like any stock, are ordered on the basis of anticipated usage. With the mechanisation of the army being so new, and indeed the widespread use of motor vehicles being far from old, there was little data to go on. The problem was made worse by the lack of experienced drivers – the loss and damage to vehicles was described as 'astronomical'.[44] Many of us knew people who 'learnt to drive in the war'. It is clear that much of this learning was from mistakes rather than anything resembling a system of training.

Another parts-related issue stemmed from the fact that a good many vehicles had been bought piecemeal and so it was barely practical to stock the necessary huge range of spares in field depots. Damaged vehicles require repair. The workshop provision of the BEF was initially grossly inadequate. A letter to the Quartermaster General dated 17 September gives a sense of the scale of provision that mechanisation would require:

Motorcycle training in gas masks for BEF. (RLC Museum)

It is not necessary for me to point out how much this completely mechanised force depends upon the efficiency of its repair organisation and my estimate of our minimum requirement for the Base Ordnance Workshop is 135,000 sq. ft ... Within six months in any event, and much earlier if operations begin, this figure will require to be increased three or four times ... In the meantime there is a grave risk of a breakdown in the Ordnance Repair organisation ... To overcome this risk I suggest the French authorities be requested to make available for 6 months two complete engineering works, to be approved by me, of a total area not less than half a million square feet.[45]

In the case of field workshops the problem was again one of learning, since there was no previous experience of carrying our repairs on such a scale. Lessons learnt would prove vital in later campaigns.

DEPOTS

Location was also to prove a major problem. Some time had been spent in reconnaissance to identify appropriate sites for depots. Bill Williams recounted a story of going over to France with a number of other officers in 'civvies' and being amused by the lengths to which one of the officers would go not to arouse suspicion, which, of course, had quite the opposite effect.

In the event, the RAOC found the premises made available by the French woefully inadequate. In Nantes they were allocated a former factory, whose floors were strewn with broken glass, and a large number of other smaller buildings dotted around the town. These buildings, with the addition of some others, became 1 Base Ordnance Depot (BOD), which would hold vehicles and stores under the command of Colonel Palmer, who would later create the major new depot at Bicester. Nantes was also the location for the Base Ordnance Workshop for major vehicle repairs.[46]

In due course, with the navy's command of the Channel, the possibility arose for a second depot near Le Havre. The COO, Dickie Richards, made perhaps his first mark on the war by taking the initiative in managing, by direct contact with the president of the Compagnie Générale Transatlantique, to obtain use of the Gare Maritime. Le Havre became 2 BOD, holding general stores and clothing.[47]

J.K. Stanford tells, in his account of his war with the RAOC, how he joined 2 BOD at Didcot and oversaw the loading of stores on to the ship which would take them across the Channel:

Motorcycle training for BEF. (RLC Museum)

Field workshop, BEF. (RLC Museum)

For two days the loading went on, a leisurely and astonishingly haphazard process. Our unmilitary goods ranged from Lister trucks and filing cabinets to typewriters and boot repairing machines. I watched three dockers, one with his boot cut wide open because of gout and all veterans long past their prime, edging wooden crates gingerly off a pile till the top crate crashed from the truck roof to the floor, then from the floor to the wharf.[48]

It seems that many crates were not up to this sort of handling and had to be bound up with string until they eventually made it into the hold. Stanford's account is run through with a strong thread of cynicism. However, the shortcomings in the practices of shipment were to repeat themselves in the later campaigns in North Africa. Once he arrived at the Quai Transatlantique, Stanford recalls being asked for 400 tons of steel racking which were meant to be on-board ship. On finding that there was none, he was told, 'My God, won't Dickie be wild?'

Stanford replied, asking, 'Who's Dickie?'

'Our COO and a cyclone in human shape if ever there was one. He's been cursing Didcot about that blasted racking for a month.' As Director

Dickie Richards and Bill Williams relaxing.

of Clothing and Equipment working closely with Bill Williams, Dickie Richards was later given oversight of Didcot.

The problem of co-ordination of field operations and UK depots continued to tax minds right up until the preparation for D-Day.

Stanford offers a wonderful description of the accommodation at the Gare Maritime. He explains that it was built by the Germans as a reparation in 1920 and possessed a 'teutonic spaciousness and austerity. With steel doors, imitation marble floors and windows set so that nobody could see out of them, it was a blend of cathedral and railway waiting room.' His account is disarming in its normality; it is hard to imagine that a war might be going on, or at least about to start. This is writ large with his account of being sent back to England on 9 May to buy kit for the cricket team; it seems that someone had taken the lease of a sports ground but had omitted to buy anything with which to play. He is thoroughly damning of what he saw as an enormous number of non-combatant troops, the tail of the army: a bone of contention that would continue to haunt the RAOC.

AMMUNITION

Ammunition is generally stored separately from other equipment and initially two Base Ammunition Depots (BADs) were set up in forests in the north-west of France, Forêt du Gâvre near Nantes and Plouaret, east of Brest. The forest location achieved the objective of camouflage but at the cost of accessibility. By May 1940 three further BADs had been added, the most forward at Rouen and one dedicated to chemical weapons at Fécamp, in the event that the Germans opted for chemical attack.

Ammunition was also an area that suffered from a desperate shortage of trained men and this imposed a huge burden on those older men who had seen action in the Great War.[49] Plan 'A' of the BEF was to form a defensive line on the Belgian border supplied from depots secured miles away from possible attack. The downside to this plan soon became apparent with the distances that both ammunition and stores had to travel. In the case of stores, the RAOC had initially to beg space on RASC lorries, although in time they did secure their own transport.

Also, partly to counter the problem of distance, railhead depots were set up. Ammunition trains were preloaded so that there was always nine days' supply in the pipeline. The use of rail really replicated the supply plan from the First World War, and experience soon showed that with highly mobile armies this no longer worked.

RAOC AND RASC

The problem of the need for the RAOC to 'beg and borrow' stemmed from the way in which the corps was regarded and, in turn, the way in which the corps had come to regard itself in the interwar years. It was non-combatant, its officers were not eligible for Staff College, it was excluded from planning and its training was separate from the army as a whole.[50] In contrast, the RASC, which also came under the control of the Quartermaster General and was responsible for food, fuel and transport, was more fully integrated. This difference manifested itself, for example, where the RAOC needed to transport supplies and were told that no transport was available. Both Bill and Dickie were acutely aware of the problem, but also of the deeply entrenched attitudes that would need to be shaken before any change would come.

Nevertheless, the story of the way the RAOC mechanised the British Army in the Second World War would be seriously incomplete without proper mention of the RASC. This corps had the principal responsibility for transportation, whether by rail, road or coastal ship. It supplied the fuel the vehicles would use, but also that which would be used by fighting vehicles such as tanks. Until 1942 it also supplied the food to feed the troops. The RASC was later responsible for the operation of Mulberry harbours in Normandy and the PLUTO pipeline under the ocean, which was laid across the Channel to supply the invading forces with fuel. That, however, was a number of years into the future. In 1940, like everyone else, the RASC was still discovering the challenges of mechanised warfare.

ASSESSMENTS OF THE BEF

If the whole situation endured by the BEF strikes the reader as faintly ludicrous, the official history of the war in France and Flanders 1939–40 shows that it was not inconsistent with the overall picture.

> The six months that followed are unique in the history of modern warfare. Germany had attacked Poland and, because of this, Britain and France had declared war on Germany. It was a brave act, for neither country was equipped for such a fight, and other free nations applauded as the Allies mobilised their forces and arranged them for battle on the French frontier.
>
> And then we waited. We waited whilst Germany conquered Poland and divided the spoils with Russia. We waited whilst Germany moved her armies to the west and disposed them to attack us. We waited, then, for

Hitler to choose the time and place for his assault. And while we waited, the applause of a world which could not know how ill-prepared we were, changed into astonishment as Germany was allowed to mass her armies without interference on the western frontier while the Allies prepared to defend themselves.[51]

In April 1940, the Controller of Ordnance Services (COS), Major General Basil Hill, visited the BEF. The visit was a follow-up to the report of the Bruce-Lewis Committee, which had found many shortcomings. In particular, it found that by February 1940, as a result of a number of factors (not least the very severe winter weather), some 40 per cent of the BEF's equipment was undergoing repair in RAOC and RASC workshops. The committee had recommended the closer working of the base workshops but also that more extensive repair should be relegated to workshops in the United Kingdom, much in line with William Rootes' earlier findings. A system of major repair in the UK would also help to reduce the range of spare parts kept at overseas workshops. This also remained a challenge throughout the war.

Hill was also critical of a number of other areas, not least the Returned Stores Depot at 2 BOD. This was to have been of great significance in the campaign with detailed plans for the extensive recovery and reuse of stores. In the event, this was never tested. Another major shortcoming was the 5,000 'to follow' vouchers in the Motor Transport Sub-depot. These represented items that could not be delivered from England because they hadn't been received from manufacturers. Hill's action point was to press the Ministry of Supply. On the plus side, Hill reported how well the Chilwell Visidex system of control and accounting was working. He added, however, 'the system will only produce real value when fully implemented'. The report is some twenty pages long. There is nothing to say how much had been actioned before the evacuation.[52]

NORWAY

While the BEF was waiting on the Belgian border, another theatre was opening, albeit briefly. The decision had been taken to invade Norway to try to avoid it falling into German hands as Denmark had done. Two points of attack were chosen and, again, there was no involvement from members of the corps in the planning. The first attack on Trondheim had a small RAOC contingent under the command of Lieutenant Colonel Cobb and Lieutenant Colonel Cutforth (the latter would play a key part in D-Day). It suffered from the non-arrival of stores, some having been destroyed en route by German aircraft, and an insufficiency of both vehicles and manpower. In order to avoid total disaster, the force was evacuated on 1 and 3 May. The episode led to a vote of censure in the House of Commons that the government won, but which began the process that would install Winston Churchill as Prime Minister.[53]

The other point of attack was Narvik. Here the corps did succeed in setting up a detachment base ordnance depot under the command of Lieutenant Colonel T.H. Clark, who would take the lead ordnance role with the 2nd Army on D-Day. Here, efforts were thwarted by a combination of very low temperatures and stores packed and documented in a way wholly unsuited for use in the field. This force was also evacuated, this time on 8 June.

ACTION AND RETREAT IN FRANCE

The wait for the BEF in France came to an end on 10 May. RAOC soldier Ernie Man recalled the rush of activity:[54]

At Lindenbook we unloaded and set up office, but after a few hours we were told to load up and move to another location, and this was the norm from then on, never staying anywhere for more than 24 hours, moving at all hours of the day and night, sleeping in barns and fields and always under the constant threat of air attack.

Despite all the shortcomings and difficulties the corps had faced over the winter, by dint of hard work and constant training the ordnance operation functioned well as the initial German attack was held.

The plan for the BEF, and indeed the French, had been based on the impregnability of the defensive Maginot line on the French border. When the Germans broke through at Sedan in the Ardennes the Allies were taken by surprise, for it had been thought of as impenetrable.

A key but unexpected role was taken by the newly formed Auxiliary Military Pioneer Corps. This unit had as its principal role the provision of labour in support of Ordnance, RASC and Engineers; in former incarnations it had been known as the Labour Corps. In 1939 it was put together using Reservists from both infantry and cavalry. These men were largely untrained and they came to France with no expectation of fighting. These were, perhaps, some of the non-combatant troops that Stanford had so clearly taken against. They came into their own when the German Panzers broke through the Allied line on 14 May, since they were some of the few troops

between it and the Channel coast, other British and French divisions being committed in Belgium. The Pioneers were equipped as best as they could be from the advanced ordnance depot.[55] They played a vital part in enabling the withdrawal that followed. Right through the war the Pioneer Corps, as they became known in November 1940, would work hand-in-hand with the RAOC both in the field and at home depots.

Attack by enemy aircraft was an ever-present risk in the retreat to Dunkirk. Colonel (then Major) P.R. Hill wrote to his wife from 2nd Ordnance Field Park BEF on 25 May 1940:[56]

The continued fine weather favours the blasted German airforce whilst our own is attacking his lines of communication or sitting at home kept there by windy politicians. Tell John Sulley we want fighters and yet more fighters. If they appear the Germans simply can't stand up to them.

He also wrote about the terrible behaviour of the Germans to the streams of refugees and how 'we are fighting for our very existence'.

One key to the success of the retreat must lie, at least in part, with the Anti-Aircraft Brigade and the effectiveness of that brigade was in turn at least in part due to the effectiveness of the RAOC repair workshops. An extract from an account of the retreat of 'A' Section, 1st Brigade Workshop gives a sense of what it might have been like:[57]

On receipt of the news that Holland had been invaded, plan 'D' was put into operation and all outstanding work was cleared up. This included assembly of a Ford V8 engine and two Leyland Terrier Engines which had been stripped down for complete overhaul. A Humber with clutch cable trouble and two motor cycles had also been repaired ... by 1800 all work in hand had been completed and returned to units and at 1830 hours the workshop moved off ... two bombing raids were encountered but no damage done ... Workshops were established in a large barn and surrounding buildings at Arbres ... Extensive repairs were carried out to a Bofors gun which had overturned ... two Bren Gun Emplacements were dug to defend the workshops ... many bombing attacks were experienced.

At Romarin a big amount of gun work was completed. One 3.7 inch AA gun was completely rewired.

On 28 May orders were received to destroy and dump the majority of our vehicles.

29 May in the afternoon we were again heavily shelled and moved into the sand dunes behind La Panne ... at 2200 hours with 17th AA

Battery (the last operating) and Regiment HQ moved to the racecourse at Dunkirk … the remainder of the vehicles were destroyed and the party marched with personal weapons and two Bren guns in good order onto the mole at Dunkirk and embarked on a destroyer at 2100 hours arriving Dover at 0450 hours on 2 June.

It was a heart rending process. I saw one particular sergeant who had tended his specialised equipment vehicle with loving care who was in tears when we smashed costly equipment with the sledge hammers we wielded … we slashed tyres, ran engines until they seized up, put sugar in the fuel tanks and hammered cylinder blocks.

Later, we made our way to the cooks' lorry for an issue of stew. We were told it was the last meal to be served, but were each given a tin of bully beef and a packet of biscuits and told to make it last …

Alwyn Ward's[58] expertise was the repair of guns. He tells how, following the invasion of Holland on 10 May, his workshop was ordered to move to Armentières. The field workshop personnel travelled by coach, in contrast to the infantry they saw en route who had to march along the roads (so much for mechanisation!) By 20 May, refugees were flooding the roads in both directions and stray dogs, left behind by those trying to escape the German advance, were becoming a problem. Orders were given to shoot them. There was little gun repair work but colleagues were kept busy with vehicle repairs.

When the order came to retreat they went first to Bergues and then to Warhem, where orders were given for vehicles and stores to be destroyed. That was Monday, 27 May. Alwyn had to wait until Friday, 31 May before he finally made it to Dover and food.

The long wait in the sand dunes witnessed periods of chaos when Stukas attacked without mercy, then periods of quiet order as men formed long queues to wait for the small ships that covered the sea under an overcast sky. Some of his mates found bottles of wine in a deserted house. They suffered more than he when the water ran out, dry mouths and hangovers compounding fear and hunger. On the penultimate day, exhausted and getting beyond hunger, a group including Alwyn was called to carry a stretcher holding a private who had been wounded fighting the rearguard action just outside Dunkirk. They joined other stretcher parties making their way along the Mole amid falling shells. They somehow made it to the hospital ship and could then join the queue for their own rescue on HMS *Codrington*.

Private Eric Avery wrote to his brother on 28 June 1940 telling of his experience as part of the 7th Advance Field Workshop. As with other accounts, it is a story of setting up and for ever moving on. At one point he talks of moving some 12km inside Belgium to a place of no military significance 'until we arrived'. They eventually made it to Dunkirk and took cover in the cellar of a butcher's shop. Information was sparse or non-existent and they decided to head for the beach through what turned out to be 2 miles of destroyed town. Their commander, Lieutenant Colonel Bell, was killed by material flying from a bursting bomb.

They spent the night in the ruins of a house near the beach. The following morning, a sailor arrived at 7 a.m. and said that a destroyer was waiting at the end of the jetty and would take them if they were prepared to risk running for it under fire. They took their chance and, under fire from the air and followed by a U-boat, they made it back to Dover. From there they were put on trains and ended up scattered around the country. Private Avery ends his letter by saying, 'we are doing nothing at all to help the country. Some have applied to reinstatement in their civilian jobs.'[59]

In his book, *Blood, Tears and Folly*, Len Deighton quotes a Royal Artillery officer's eyewitness account of what happened to equipment on the evacuation:

It was now that I saw for the first time regiments in the doleful process of wrecking their equipment. New wireless sets, costing perhaps £20 apiece, were placed in rows in fields, twenty in a row sometimes, while a soldier with a pick-axe proceeded up and down knocking them to pieces. Trucks were being dealt with just as dramatically. Radiators and engines were smashed with sledge-hammers; tyres slashed and sawn after they had been deflated. Vehicles that were near the canals were finally pushed in. Some of the canals were choked with the wrecks, all piled on top of each other.

He then quotes a German officer writing home saying, 'there were hundreds, possibly thousands, of cars, trucks armoured vehicles of all sizes. Almost all of them were burnt out, because the British and French had put fire to all vehicles they had abandoned … there was a vast amount of war materiel, all useless.' In simple numbers, Deighton states that the BEF had abandoned 2,472 guns and 63,879 vehicles and more than half a million tons of supplies.

While most of the equipment left behind was unusable, it could all be subjected to investigation by the German technical men. This would have revealed no great strength in armaments but it would have given them vital clues as to how the British motor industry might develop its vehicles from then on.

Beneath Deighton's 'simple' numbers there lies a more complex story. It seems that the War Office couldn't make up its mind what to do with the Le Havre BOD. On the one hand there was a need to get equipment back to England following the successful evacuation at Dunkirk, but set against this was the political imperative of showing support to the French and having equipment for any British troops who would continue to fight alongside them. The base was eventually abandoned and with it, as Stanford says, much equipment, 'a mountain of stores and clothing, 990,000 greatcoats and a million pairs of boots, which no British soldier would wear, and accommodation stores beyond all counting. They were simply too bulky to be reloaded and returned.'

The position with the Nantes Depot was a little different since, from the time of the first withdrawal, Colonel Palmer had been sending valuable warlike stores back over the Channel.[60] Given its position a good way from the German advance there was more time for an orderly evacuation. Tragically, however, an even greater disaster awaited.

On 17 June some 6,000 soldiers and airmen, including the remaining 200 ordnance personnel, boarded SS *Lancastria*, a 17,000-ton former Cunard Liner. Just as it was heading out to sea, Stukas struck and it sank within fifteen minutes with the loss of 2,000 lives, including fifty ordnance men. Tragic though this was, the greater loss was of RAF ground crew who had boarded first and who were 'crammed like sardines' under deck.

Kitchens at COD Chilwell.

Jack Lumsden survived by jumping into the sea and swimming free. He went on to serve at Chilwell, Derby and Burton, retiring as a major after thirty-seven years with the RAOC. Douglas Hanson was another RAOC survivor from the *Lancastria*. He recalled the enemy machine-gunning survivors and also the lack of lifebelts. He suffered burns from the burning oil on the surface of the sea; it took some ten weeks before he was ready to return to service.

Many people played a part in caring for the troops as they arrived back home from Dunkirk. COD Chilwell welcomed some 7,000 evacuated troops. Sergeant Major Hall of the ATS recalls them arriving:

> We gave them bacon and eggs and lashings of hot tea and when they'd finished they just fell asleep at the table. Everyone came to Building 176 to cook, serve, wash dishes … the commanding officer and the newest recruit rolled up their sleeves and worked side-by-side; our men gave up their cigarettes and chocolate and beds, handed over some of their own clothes and did any odd jobs they could …[61]

Doris Smith was one of the cooks. She came from South Shields where, before the war, she had been a housekeeper. When war was declared she had volunteered, choosing the ATS rather than the WRNS because she 'didn't like water'. Her shock on arriving at Chilwell was at the sheer volume of food to be cooked. The arrival of the Dunkirk evacuees tripled the number of mouths to be fed. She recalled having to step over sleeping body after sleeping body as she tried to cross one of the massive sheds to wake the stoker so that the kitchen ranges could be ready to cook thousands of breakfasts. A later memory of that summer was being handed a pair of binoculars and a tin hat and being sent up to the roof of one of the sheds to look out for enemy planes. She arrived as a shy country girl, but her experience at Chilwell gave her the confidence to pursue a successful career in catering.[62]

Although by far the majority of British troops were evacuated, some thousands, mainly those charged with fighting a rearguard action, were taken prisoner. Wilfred Beeson[63] had transferred to 14th Army Field Workshop. His unit had been caught in a pincer movement at Saint Martin although he had managed to escape, taking refuge in the belfry of the local church. He was cared for by the nuns until it became too dangerous. He moved on to try to join the 51st Highland Division, which was fighting at St Valerie, but was captured and joined some 6,000 British and French prisoners. He recalls his interrogator boasting about capturing equipment and saying that Churchill and the British Government had evacuated to Canada. Wilfred's patriotic remonstration earned him some harsh handling. He then joined an even larger column of 15,000 British and French troops as they marched for twenty-one days virtually non-stop with no proper provision for food or shelter. He recalls the kindness of the French women throwing them crusts of bread.

James Welford[64] was also with 14th Ordnance Field Workshop. On 19 May they were ordered to retreat to Saint-Omer where, after three days, they were surrounded and taken prisoner. They were marched for two or three days with neither food nor water, sweating by day, freezing by night. James was taken ill with dysentery but soon was herded into a cattle truck and in excessive heat and filth made the journey to Toruń in Poland. The Polish winter subjected the prisoners to temperatures of -40°C and many suffered frostbite. James' boots fell apart and he was given wooden clogs and 'foot rags'. They were permanently hungry and suffered terribly from bed lice. Red Cross parcels did come through and were the saving grace; Russian and Ukrainian prisoners who had to survive only on camp rations died by the hundreds.

In 1942 they were moved to a better equipped camp in Heydebreck, close to a factory producing fuel for V-1s and V-2s. While life was better, in 1944 another, more deadly, threat emerged with massive attacks from USAF B-17 bombers. James survived, many more didn't. Many bombs fell in the neighbouring forest and inmates from Auschwitz were sent to seek out the deadly loads. With the advance of the Americans, the British prisoners of war (POWs) were marched further into Poland, the agony of the march only made easier when compared to the female inmates of Auschwitz marching more slowly and in much greater agony. They were finally liberated by General Patton's advancing army.

The BEF cost many lives and much materiel. One particular loss for ordnance was in the shape of experienced non-commissioned officers (NCOs) who had been killed or taken prisoner. Aside from the human aspect, these men had gained rare skills which would have to be replaced. Lessons, too, had been learnt as is evident from the final despatch of the commander-in-chief:

> The days are past when armies can be hurriedly raised, equipped and placed in the field, for modern war demands the ever-increasing use of complex material … modern equipment requires time to design and produce, and once it is produced, further time is required to train troops in its technical and tactical uses. Improvised arrangements, made at short notice, can only lead to the shortage of essential equipment, the production of inferior articles, and the unskilful handling of weapons and vehicles in the battlefield.[65]

THE UK MOTOR INDUSTRY

By the early summer of 1940, the British motor companies were working at full tilt producing everything from aircraft, ammunition parts and tin hats to a vast array of military vehicles. The vehicles that had crossed the Channel with the BEF had been largely adaptions of commercial vans and trucks. However, in the spring of 1940 members of the General Staff, with leaders of the motor industry, had gone over to France to see how their vehicles were performing in the field. It had been a wake-up call all round and they returned with a much clearer focus on what was needed. The experience of the ensuing years would add to this focus as better and more suitable vehicles were produced. For example, scout cars had originated in 1938 but experience of the BEF resulted in more heavily armed versions that proved their value in later campaigns.

In short, in May 1940 it was going well. Then came Dunkirk.

No one dismisses the human tragedy, or indeed the triumph of the flotilla of little ships, but for all those who had laboured so hard to mechanise the army, it was a body blow. It is difficult to say how the thousands of men, and now women, working in the motor industry felt. Sickened at the loss? Overwhelmed by the task that lay ahead? Determined to play their part? Certainly fearful of invasion and the dreadful picture that had been painted of the reality of bombing raids.

The trade press of the time put on rather more than a brave face. The leading article in the *Commercial Motor* of 15 June 1940 adopted a strongly belligerent tone, reminding the Nazis that with only 6 per cent of the world they would not prevail. The losses of men and materiel were acknowledged but were said to be much lower than the German losses to date.[1] With the benefit of hindsight, in the same magazine of 10 September 1943 Mr A.F. Phillips, president of SMMT, said:

> Our position at the time of Dunkirk was such that the troops then in Britain were largely unarmed and without ammunition. We had only 46 tanks, mostly obsolete. Only a production miracle could have saved the position and the motor industry took a vital part in performing the kind of miracle required.

This chapter is an account of that miracle.

Lord Beaverbrook had been appointed Minister for Aircraft Production on 14 May 1940. This was not in time to have any impact on the BEF but it contributed significantly to the resourcing of the RAF for the Battle of Britain. With most motor companies already heavily involved in aircraft manufacture and repair, the 'hotting-up of the pace' that resulted from the appointment spread throughout the industry. Beaverbrook later became Minster of Supply and then Minister of War Production, posts which gave him a direct influence over tank production.

The British Motor Industry had been put on war alert at the declaration of war. They had ceased domestic production and awaited orders from the ministries. For a few, orders came quickly; for many there was nothing and factories lay silent. In time orders did come, but in what can only be described as a torrent of unco-ordinated demands. Ministries requested aircraft parts and ammunition; they needed helmets; they gave instructions for the development of new vehicles; they demanded cars cut in half with ambulance bodies replacing what had been in the rear. Factory managers must have wondered who was running the war; nevertheless, they coped.

THE CHALLENGE

With the return of the BEF minus some 64,000 vehicles, needs became urgent, as is underlined by the statistic in Charles Graves's book, *Drive for Freedom*. In June 1940 there were only forty-six obsolete tanks and forty or fifty light armoured cars that had been returned to England for repair.[2] Graves tells that all vehicles had been replaced in 120 days. Alan Fernyhough, in his *History of the RAOC 1918–1945*, observed that the rush to produce resulted in a fall in quality and increased unreliability.[3] Whichever way you look at it, the British motor industry faced, and met, a huge challenge, not least because its role had expanded to include much more than vehicles, and its skilled manpower base had been reduced. Although in protected occupations, many manufacturers had lost key skilled men to the army, many to the RAOC.

The demands for production rose, however, and so a new workforce was needed. 'Green' labour was recruited, mainly women, and they all needed training, which placed yet further burdens on the older craftsmen. The evidence is that they rose to the challenge and the new workforce proved itself to be as good as, and in many cases better than, the ones who had left for war. The results were positive, with motivated workforces exceeding targets. Nevertheless, none of this was without its social impact:

Most of the girls who came to Morris Commercial were from remote farms and villages in Scotland. They settled down well enough in the factory, but in the evenings when they trooped out into the crowded and blacked-out pavements of Birmingham, they felt quite bewildered. It was not easy to overcome the feeling of homesickness.

Torn suddenly from their secluded life and home ties, a few girls abandoned themselves to evenings of gaiety. Peevish landladies would appear at the factory next morning to complain to the welfare supervisor that their boarders had arrived home too late. The supervisor would then confront the girl with the landlady, a new billet would be found, and after a little dramatic scene, things usually went smoothly.[4]

THE VEHICLES

The range of vehicles produced for the war effort was staggering and cumbersome. Just about all the peacetime manufacturers rose to the challenge, as did their subcontractors and specialist suppliers. The RAOC distinguished between 'A' (armoured) vehicles and 'B' vehicles (essentially everything else). With the exception of tanks and some very heavy vehicles, most manufacturers made both types plus a great deal of other war materiel.

The Austin Motor Company at Longbridge, south of Birmingham, famous for the Austin 7, manufactured some 120,000 military vehicles of all kinds ranging from the 8hp utility vehicles to 3-ton trucks, importantly also used as recovery trucks. In 1939 Austin had planned to re-enter the commercial vehicle market with a 30cwt truck. With mobilisation this evolved into the Austin 2-ton truck, of which some 27,800 were built in the Second World War, nearly half of those being the Austin K2 ambulance.[5] In addition, they produced 1.3 million rounds of 2, 6 and 7lb shells, 3.3 million ammunition boxes, 600,000 jerricans (also known as jerrycans or jerry cans) and 2.5 million steel helmets.[6]

Austin 7. (RLC Museum)

The jerrican was the product of the experience of the British Army in the desert. Petrol, and it was *only* petrol since to have some vehicles using diesel while most used petrol would have been a recipe for disaster, was carried in 5-gallon tins known as 'flimsies'. These tended to leak and were in no way robust. The German Army also used 5-gallon cans but these were strong and didn't leak. The design was 'borrowed' and millions of such cans were produced.[7]

In 1931 Ford had set up a production plant at Dagenham in East London on a 66-acre site, very much replicating the production line facilities at River Rouge in the USA. The first response by Ford to the declaration of war was the provision of Fordson tractors. Learning from the experience of the Great War that food shortages would need to be addressed, the provision of tractors to Britain's farmers was a first priority. The Ministry of Supply had been reluctant to commit to a motor vehicle supplier so susceptible to German bombing. Accordingly, steps were taken to camouflage the site with the result that no major bomb damage was suffered. The plant produced many military vehicles, particularly the popular Universal or Bren gun carrier.[8] Apart from the tractor, Fordson had begun to produce a series of 'War Office Trucks' in 1939, which it designated WOT1 to WOT6. The WOT1 was a four-wheel drive 3-ton cargo truck, of which 9,000 were produced. The WOT2 was a 15cwt two-wheel drive and some 60,000 of these were produced in the six years of the war. The WOT6 was very adaptable, being used both as a recovery vehicle and mobile workshop and store.[9] Fordson's command and staff car was the WOA2, of which 5,000 were built.[10] In total the plant produced more than 360,000 wheeled vehicles during the Second World War.

At Cowley, Morris undertook the manufacture of armoured personnel carriers, the 15cwt General Service Truck and power units. Its wheeled trucks had been developed in the early 1930s. The Morris Commercial CD 30cwt truck was produced until 1940 and its CS8 continued production until 1941, many having been left behind at Dunkirk only to be used by the Wehrmacht.[11] War correspondent Alan Moorehead reported that many of these were found among those captured in Normandy in 1944.[12] The Morris C8 4x4 was the best-known field artillery tractor of the war, also having Canadian Chevrolet and Ford equivalents.[13]

The Wolseley Company of Birmingham, also part of the Nuffield stable of motor companies, was about to produce an 8hp version of its popular Wolseley-Ten when war was declared. The factory had been tooled up for the new model and so had to be retooled to deal with the demands of war production. Morris Commercial transferred the production of the six-wheeled War Office vehicle it had been manufacturing to Wolseley, 'so allowing them to concentrate on an increased production of other vehicles for the War Office'.[14] Similarly, orders for Bren carriers, then being produced by Nuffield Mechanisations and Aero Ltd, were transferred. A total of 22,000 carriers (Bren carriers, scout carriers, universal carriers, motor carriers and Lloyd artillery tractors) were produced by Wolseley, including adaptions of carriers originally manufactured overseas.[15] An order demanding particular ingenuity was the conversion of 600 second-hand cars into ambulances.

The Wolseley factory was hit in the Birmingham bombing raids. As with the Coventry-based companies, management and workers rose to the challenge and the factory was back in production within the minimum of time.[16]

Vauxhall's principal contribution to wheeled vehicles was through the 'MW'. This had come about as a result of the War Office inviting manufacturers to produce a general service 15cwt truck. The Bedford version proved very successful, being fast with 'almost sports-car like handling'. It went on to produce 66,000 such vehicles with adaption as anti-aircraft gun tractors, machinery trucks, water carriers and radio vans.[17] The *Commercial Motor* of 6 April 1940 described the water carrier as capable of running across fields to lakes and pumping up water into the vehicle container, a mundane but vital function.

Bedford MWC model. (© Vauxhall Heritage Archive)

The Bedford QL emerged largely because the MW was not four-wheel drive and so could not work off-road. The War Office commissioned Bedford to develop this 3-ton truck, and by the end of the war 52,247 had been manufactured, again in a large number of versions.[18] Vauxhall, like Morris and others, manufactured some 5 million jerricans. Their steel-fabrication building produced much other materiel including some 4 million Venturi tubes for firing rockets.

COVENTRY

As Bill Williams had observed when he first viewed Chilwell, Coventry was home to much of the British motor industry. The reputation of the Coventry motor engineer was as familiar worldwide as that of the Cornish mining engineer.

Morris had a large engine plant in Coventry and also a body plant. In the late 1930s it built a further plant to manufacture Bofors guns from the Swedish design.

Sgt Smith and Miss Perks with Bill Williams' Humber staff car.

The first Coventry-made Bofors gun was delivered to the army on 15 June 1939 to a mixed reception. The cockney NCO who was the first to test the gun asked who the makers were:

'You're kidding,' he declared. 'It can't be Nuffield's. Don't tell me – I know – Nuffield's make motor cars. But, lumme, if this is the sort of gun they can turn out, they're doing a bit of all right.'[19]

Humber was one of the oldest Coventry motor companies. In John Bullock's history of the Rootes Group he reports with some pride that:

In 1939 the Humber Super Snipe went into battle dress and was made famous during the war by Field Marshal Montgomery, with his 'Old Faithful' and 'Victory' cars. 'Old Faithful' in particular had Thrupp and Maberly coachwork and was used by the Field Marshal throughout his North African and Sicilian campaigns.

When peace came, Monty gave the cars to Billy Rootes to thank him for the reliable service they had given throughout the hostilities.

Humber supplied staff cars for all three services.[20] The Humber FWD was a four-wheel drive, small, all-purpose vehicle based on the Humber Super Snipe. The BBC operated a fleet of these for war correspondents.[21] Karrier Motors of Luton was another company within the Rootes Group. Its K6

Gladys Barson at work at the Morris Bofors factory in Coventry.

was a four-wheel drive, 3-ton truck, of which 4,500 were produced. This, like many 3-tonners, was adaptable and was also used as a mobile workshop and store. The Humber 8cwt 4x4 Light Field Ambulance fulfilled a vital role in rescuing the wounded from the battlefields. The Humber Scout Car, also based on the Snipe, was essential equipment for almost all army divisions. The scout car and staff car were also manufactured by Daimler, another long-standing Coventry business.

Hillman was also a member of the Rootes Group, based at Ryton-on-Dunsmore close to Coventry. It produced a 5cwt 4x2 light utility, commonly known as a 'Tilly' and based on pre-war 10hp and 12hp passenger saloons, in Hillman's case the Minx which had been its best-selling model in the 1930s. Tillies were also produced by Austin at Longbridge[22], by Morris at Cowley and by Standard Cars, also in Coventry, based on the Standard Flying 14.

SS Jaguar Cars at Coventry continued to manufacture sidecars and trailers during the war, but its main contribution was in aircraft, where it made parts such as wings, cockpit roofs, bomb doors, tank formers and frames for Spitfires, Lancasters, Stirlings and Mosquitos.

With these major manufactures and a large array of subcontractors and equipment suppliers, Coventry was a busy and vital part of the war effort. On the night of 14 November 1940 disaster struck as German bombers attacked. Bombs fell over the city for a terrifying ten hours, destroying most of the housing, the cathedral and historic centre[23] but, of central interest to those concerned with war production, also causing serious damage to the Humber, Hillman and Daimler factories, the Morris Motors body factory and the Morris Motors engine factory[24] and too many subcontractors to count. A survivor remembered:

> A night of unforgettable horror – the scream of falling bombs – the shattering explosions – the showers of incendiaries, literally thousands and then – perhaps the most horrifying of all – the sudden fires leaping up, their flames, fanned by the wind, rapidly spreading and enveloping all within reach.[25]

Triumph Motorcycles had set up a factory in Coventry but this was destroyed by the bombing, having produced only fifty bikes. It relocated to Meriden in May 1942 and manufactured 49,700 machines by the end of the war. Another major motorcycle manufacturer was Norton in Birmingham, which produced some 100,000 bikes.[26] BSA, also in Birmingham, produced another 115,000.

What was most remarkable was the determination of men and management to keep production going. The spirit of Coventry was strong and production resumed amazingly quickly. Ernest Fairfax, in his book on Morris, tells of the engine factory workers operating machinery in sou'westers and gumboots after the factory roof had been blown off.[27] Coventry was attacked again in the spring of 1941, but production continued.

Billy Rootes was summoned by Prime Minister Winston Churchill to form and chair a reconstruction committee, something he did with great energy and effect. He wanted to show his workforce and the people of Coventry that they could fight back and so set out to raise £100,000 to equip a motor industry squadron of Spitfires. The aircraft were given names and the list of companies subscribing form a *Who's Who* of the wartime motor industry.[28]

The vulnerability of the motor industry to attack from the air motivated the Ministry of Supply to insist that vital production was dispersed. An important example came in the shape of the SU Carburettor Company, which not only produced carburettors for land-based vehicles, but also for many of the RAF's aircraft. The main production was moved to the south of Birmingham, with a further back-up in a former hosiery factory in Barwell in Leicestershire.

Austin Tilly. (RLC Museum)

HEAVY AND SPECIALIST VEHICLE COMPANIES

AEC at Southall in West London, the manufacturer of the world-famous London bus, turned its production in wartime to Matador and Marshall heavy trucks. These had all-wheel-drive chassis, with six pairs of wheels powered by a 120bhp engine through two gearboxes giving six speeds to all three axles. These beasts were used, among other things, for transporting pipes for the construction of oil pipelines[29] but also as a tractor for medium guns.[30]

Design work on what became the Matador was carried out by Charles Cleaver of the Four Wheel Drive Motor Company (FWD). AEC bought out FWD and Cleaver finished the design at the Southall factory. The initial contract was for 200 trucks; by the end of the war 10,500 Matadors had been produced.[31]

AEC Matador. (RLC Museum)

The Marshall was one of the vehicles used to carry mobile bridging equipment.[32] Bridging equipment vehicles[33] came in essentially two types. For small spans there were the Meccano-type parts easily transportable and erected. For larger spans there was the Bailey bridge, the variable section Hamilton Unit road bridge and the Callender-Hamilton variable section railway bridge.

Albion Motors was founded in Glasgow in 1899 and, having produced some 6,000 trucks in the Great War, manufactured a heavy artillery tractor for towing 7.2in or 6in howitzers.[34] Tank transporters[35] were produced in essentially three types: rigid chassis lorries, tractors with semi-trailers and tractors with trailers. As vehicle utilisation became more important, tractors with detachable trailers became popular, so that the tractor could deliver the tank on a trailer and immediately set off to collect another. The Albion CX 24S was a 20-ton semi-trailer and could take a Crusader.

Crossley was a Manchester company which, from the 1870s, made high-quality vehicles ranging from saloons used by royalty to buses and haulage vehicles.[36] In the Great War it had made a name for itself principally with the provision of vehicles for the Royal Flying Corps. In the interwar years, alongside other motor companies, it developed a range of trucks for military use by both Britain and India. One particular feature of Crossley was the use of Kégresse bogies,[37] making the vehicle in question a half-track and so better equipped to cope off-road. Its story between the wars reflects the arguments going on in military circles between those who wanted lightweight vehicles that could avoid getting stuck in mud, and those who favoured the strength and resilience of heavier trucks.

In 1935 the War Office, aware of developments in the USA, France and Germany in four-wheel drive, issued a specification for a Q type, 'quad' 3-tonner. Crossley developed a sophisticated version with all-round independent suspension. The pressures following Dunkirk meant that sophistication had to be put to one side, and a more straightforward version was commissioned and served alongside similar vehicles from Albion, Karrier, Austin and Bedford. Crossley remained, though, principally an RAF supplier.

Sydney Guy set up his company in Wolverhampton at the start of the Great War, having spent time with some of the great marques of the time, including Sunbeam and Humber. The coming of peace saw Guy produce a 2½-ton truck aimed at farmers with spud wheels capable of being driven over all types of terrain.[38] Guy went on to produce buses, coaches and commercial vehicles, but in 1935 they were invited to take part in

3-ton truck – a gift from India. (RLC Museum)

Leyland SWQ2 6x4. (RLC Museum)

army trials. They produced a 15cwt short wheelbase Ant which ran on low-pressure tyres.

Gun tractors[39] offer a link with their living predecessors as having to 'have good cross-country performance, be capable of carrying the gun crew and their equipment, and an initial supply of ammunition to bring the gun into operation'. The tractors break down into uses: field artillery, light anti-aircraft (Bofors) and heavy gun tractors. In 1937, Guy developed its Ant into a 4x4 Quad Ant which, for the duration of the war, would be the field artillery tractor of choice for 25-pounder guns.[40]

Derived from the design of the Quad Ant was an armoured car with revolutionary welded armour plate. The demand for this outstripped Guy's capabilities and Humber took the design and produced some thousands for the War Office.[41] This vehicle fought to great effect in the wide open space of the desert, but was found less useful in the lanes and built up areas of northern France.[42]

Leyland Motors came out of the Lancashire Steam Motor Company, and in the Great War, as with Crossley, made most of its supplies of vehicles for the Royal Flying Corps. For the army in the Second World War it adapted its 10-ton Hippo Mk II, but was late on the scene with only 1,000 being in service by VE Day. The planning for D-Day had revealed that a 10-ton truck would be more effective than the smaller capacity trucks then in use.[43] Machinery and stores[44] trucks were of essentially two types: the 'house' version with windows, perhaps too easily identified, and the general service (GS) vehicle, fully equipped inside but looking like any other GS vehicle outside. The Leyland Retriever was adapted as both a machinery and stores truck and as a recovery vehicle. Like so many motor companies, Leyland also produced bombs, shells and castings.

Scammell originated not far from Liverpool Street Station in London, where its vehicles served the local markets. In the Great War it had manufactured gun carriages and vehicle bodywork for the War Office.[45] Alfred Scammell had experienced the Great War at first hand and was definitely on the side of lighter vehicles that could avoid the dangers of mud. He favoured lighter trucks with the ability to tow trailers, thus having the same carrying ability but with a reduced weight on each axle.[46] The idea progressed into an articulated lorry which also proved popular in the commercial market. From this came the Scammell Pioneer, which performed strongly as a gun tractor or tank or machinery transporter. 'The great thing about the Pioneer was that no amount of mud or sand seemed to bog it down, although it often needed two men to handle the manual steering gear for the big front wheels.'[47] The Scammell 30-ton semi-trailer tank transporter was big enough to take a Matilda.

Scammel Pioneer. (RLC Museum)

Scammel recovery vehicle. (RLC Museum)

AEC Militant recovery
vehicle. (RLC Museum)

Mechanical horse. (RLC Museum)

Recovery vehicles[48] came in three types: those with fixed or extendable jibs, those with booms described as 'wreckers' and lastly the gantry type with a rigid steel structure. The Scammell 6x4 Heavy Breakdown was, Conniford suggests, 'probably the most widely used and longest in service of the British recovery vehicles'. The other unique Scammell contribution to RAOC work was the three-wheeled Mechanical Horse.[49]

Many other British motor companies contributed to the war effort. Foden, in Sandbach, Cheshire, manufactured a range of heavy trucks. Maudsley, at Alcester in Warwickshire, was known for its Militant 6-ton GS truck, and Thornycroft supplied some 20,000 vehicles, from mobile cranes to searchlight lorries and machine gun carriers.[50]

COMPONENT MANUFACTURERS

It wasn't just vehicle manufacturers, subcontractors and component manufacturers who played their part: Solex Carburettors, the Pyrene Company (fire extinguishers), Firestone, Triplex, Lucas, Lodge, Champion and AC Spark Plugs and Smiths Industries, to name but a few, also contributed to the war effort. Tecalamit supplied workshop equipment, and a number of officers came from Tecalamit, including Arthur Sewell, who was first at Chilwell and then took over COD Feltham in preparation for the war in the Far East.

In his history of Dunlop, James McMillan says, 'between 1939 and 1945 the Dunlop Rubber Company produced the vast majority of the 32.7 million vehicle and 47 million cycle tyres manufactured in the UK'.[51] The relationship between Dunlop and the RAOC was strong. Both Bob Hiam, COO at COD Old Dalby, and Robby Robinson, COO at COD Derby, had come from Dunlop. There is a story of a visit by a senior Dunlop delegation to Old Dalby and how they took away many new ideas on organisation from the techniques developed within the RAOC.

The car battery, to us in the twenty-first century, is enclosed, reliable and clean. In the middle of the twentieth century, even though technology had made great strides forward, the battery, with its elements suspended in acid, was far from simple. Oldham[52] produced a great many batteries for army vehicles in the Second World War, gaining a reputation for reliability. The problems in the mining industry had encouraged a shift towards the more buoyant motor industry so Oldham had been well prepared when war came.

GARAGES ACROSS THE COUNTRY

In towns and villages around the country, garages large and small found that many of their mechanics had joined up. This was initially a blessing as domestic motor use had declined, and with it the need for repairs. Many businesses found they had capacity and the more entrepreneurial approached the Ministry of Supply. At first they were met with a bureaucratic 'no', then, with the Blitz, dispersal had become the order of the day and the result was the awarding of contracts for war work. One London garage repaired the vehicles of the 51st Division before it embarked for North Africa. Others manufactured parts for munitions and some whole shells. Army vehicles were repaired and serviced, mainly light armoured cars and Bren carriers but, in fact, a huge range of different work was undertaken.

In time, workforces expanded and with so many men in the armed forces many garages, like the major manufacturers, recruited women, who soon gained the necessary skills from the careful teaching of those, mostly older, skilled men left behind.

There was a shortage of machine tools and many garages made their own, suitable for use by relatively unskilled labour, using the parts they had to hand. The same was true of spare parts, where, for example, those coming from the USA were lost in sunk Atlantic convoys; these too were manufactured on the workbenches of garages, large and small, urban and rural. One London firm equipped LCVs (lorry command vehicles), which would be the Signals HQ in the field. Another developed a tool to counter the adverse effect of the reduced viscosity of oil in guns in the desert.

Graves[53] quotes the Right Honourable Colonel Llewellyn's words of praise on behalf of the government:

> It is just as well that a tribute should be paid … to those who work in the smaller firms, because up and down the country, wherever you may go and wherever you may look, it is these smaller firms, almost without exception, who have played just as full a part, according to their capacity, as have the larger firms.

THE TANK

On 28 October 1941 Bill Williams was invited to give the response to the toast at the Worshipful Company of Carmen, the City of London livery company for the motor distribution industry. He began by apologising for the insatiable demands he was placing on motor manufactures for both new vehicles and spare parts. He then went on to talk about the problems of tank production, explaining that this was the area of latest development for the 'Army Carmen business':

There is not only the tank itself, but the guns, the machine guns, the wireless which has to operate under the most difficult conditions, and stand up to incredibly rough treatment, and many other things as well – watches, binoculars, sighting instruments and other secret devices of all sorts. All these are items of extreme delicacy in design and manufacture and need skilled hands to make them. All these different articles of equipment have to be married together in our Ordnance Depots before the tank can be issued to the troops or fighting unit ... There must be no mistakes. Everything must be of the best, the best armour-plating, the best guns, the best engines, power operated turrets, the best wireless, the best that the Ministry of Supply and the great engineering industry of this country can produce ... Even when the tank has been completely assembled, has left the depot, and joined its unit, we still have to look after it. A tank, for all its strength, is a delicate instrument of war. It requires constant attention.

The tanks of which Bill Williams spoke were those produced largely after Dunkirk. The Vickers Valentine, ordered by the War Office on St Valentine's Day 1939, and hence possibly the inspiration for the name,[54] was produced in great numbers: 8,275 being a quarter of all British wartime tank production. The British version was used in the western desert and almost 1,400 of the Canadian version were sent to Russia.[55] It again was developed for other uses. The Valentine could carry a 17lb gun, which made it a fearsome weapon. The success of this tank lay also in its heavy armour and its use of the tried and tested AEC engine, as fitted in London buses. The use of other tried and tested parts added to its reliability.[56] In contrast, the Vickers light tank was used to little effect in the desert, Greece and Crete. Its little successor, the Tetrarch, was flown in by glider to support airborne troops landing on D-Day.[57]

In late 1937, Nuffield Mechanisation was set up in a factory close to the Birmingham Wolseley works and became the only plant in Britain to make complete tanks under one roof. The Nuffield approach to tank production was adopted by the very large number of subcontractors and other motor manufactures who became involved in the tank project. One issue that caused Nuffield major headaches was the type of engine that was available. The horsepower tax had pushed engine designers away from large powerful engines towards small, high-revving, long stroke models quite unsuited to the needs of the heavy tank. This shortcoming was addressed initially by the use of the old American Liberty engine.

From the Nuffield stable came a series of tanks, each with advantages and drawbacks, the latter becoming apparent only as the enemy upped their game. The most famous of these in the early part of the war was the Crusader, of which some 5,300 were built and which overpowered the Italians in the desert, but not the Germans. The Cromwell, which was in many ways the successor to the Crusader, was the first British tank with a welded hull. It was powered by a Rolls-Royce Meteor engine which made it fast, with a top speed of 40mph. It did, though, come on to the scene at the same time as the American Sherman. The Centurion was the successor to the Cromwell, but came into service too late for the Second World War. It was said to perform well in all three attribute areas.

Leyland was part of the network of companies which joined together in the development of the tank. A Leyland engine powered the Matilda, and Leyland worked with others on the Centaur and Cromwell and designed and built the Comet,[58] which, with its 77mm gun, would lead the crossing of the Rhine and the final drive into Germany. Also part of the network of tank builders was the Birmingham Railway Carriage and Wagon Co. Ltd. They also manufactured the Hamilcar glider which would carry tanks and airborne troops into France.[59]

Vauxhall had contributed to the development of existing tanks, but they were then asked to design and manufacture a brand new and more powerful engine of 350bhp, vastly greater than the smaller high-revving Bedford engines currently in production. A new test bed had to be built, and the prototype of the new engine was running only eighty-nine days after the request had been made. The Ministry of Supply then decided that it needed a very much heavier tank and Vauxhall were commissioned to design and build it.

In his account of Vauxhall during the Second World War, W.J. Seymour is at pains to point out that no self-respecting engineer would produce a brand new vehicle without extensive testing and a whole sequence of prototypes. However, England after Dunkirk was in a desperate hurry to get into a position where it could stand up to Germany. The Churchill, as it was called, was put into production. It was not a success on day one, but rather developed through modification into a machine that did the job. Vauxhall were developing a successor when hostilities ceased. The Churchill was perhaps best known for the many ways in which it was adapted, from flame-thrower to bridge transport and anti-mine flail.[60] The Churchill

Matilda tanks
at COD
Chilwell.

Mk III, with special engine pipes to enable them to 'wade' in water up to the top of the hull,[61] was deployed on the ill-fated Dieppe raid and, being unable to cope with the steep shingle beach, had to remain behind – Britain's latest tank left for the German Army.[62]

As Bill Williams had observed, it was one thing to make a tank but they also demanded significant maintenance:

A Churchill tank engine weighs two tons and contains 4,000 different parts. The holdings to keep a squadron of Churchills alone are immense. For Landing Reserves one hundred Churchills require one hundred and ninety tons of spare parts to cover a period of only fourteen days.[63]

TOO MANY MODELS

Over the five years of the war, the number of different vehicles grew almost exponentially. Charles Graves puts it like this, referring especially to the tank:

> Since 1939, under the stress of wartime conditions, a whole sequence of tanks has been developed. Beginning with the Matilda, of which there have been five designs to date, and the Valentine, of which there have been eleven, there are the Crusader with four designs, the Covenanter, the Centaur, the Cromwell with seven designs, and the Churchill with eight. On top of that, there have been six types of light tank, nine types of reconnaissance car, scout car and armoured car, together with 350 types of army lorries, and all kinds of armoured recovery vehicle.

The reasons for the huge variety of different vehicles can now only be guessed at. I would venture that one reason might be cultural. In his book, *The Industry-Ordnance Team*, Bill's American opposite number Lewin Campbell wrote, 'Ordnance is responsible for the design and development of the vast majority of the weapons, ammunition and automotive vehicles of our fighting forces'. This resulted in common specifications and therefore common spare parts. This may well have come from the Henry Ford dictum, 'any colour you want so long as it's black'. This contrasts with the craftsmen-based UK motor industry and the tradition of the gifted amateur engineer and boffin. To them, variations were seen as challenges to be tackled with relish rather than inconveniences that got in the way of efficiency. I suggest that the suppliers were only too keen to oblige when the army chiefs demanded this or that variation. In between came the Ministry and endless committees – in four years, no fewer than four ministers of war, surely not a recipe for efficiency.

This is no way detracts from the magnificent way in which the motor industry served the country in wartime, indeed, it makes it all the more commendable that they delivered as much as they did. It does make clear, however, the enormous task of organisation that faced the RAOC.

THE DEPOTS AND MECHANISATION

The British Army that returned from France was exhausted, dispirited and no longer mechanised in any real sense. The stark reality in the summer of 1940 was that at some point Hitler would invade these islands. Accordingly, the army set up, within what was really a peacetime structure of area commands, a Home Army alongside a vital anti-aircraft command. By July 1940, by hook or by crook, some five divisions had been re-equipped by the small, largely civilian-manned ordnance depots within each area command. These were supported by the five existing central ordnance depots. In addition to Chilwell, there were depots dating from the Great War at Woolwich (armaments), Bramley (ammunition), Weedon (small arms) and Didcot (clothing and general stores).[1]

Wally Harris[2] was posted to the LAD attached to the 90th City of London Field Regiment. Those units that had been left behind now came into their own as they assumed responsibility, in Wally's case, to share in the defence of Southern England. They began to receive the equipment they needed and requisitioned commercial garages to supplement army resources. Each LAD was led by an armament sergeant major, a man of experience who taught his soldiers and also his officers how to be 'soldier smart'. They learnt from each other how best to carry out their duties as a LAD. There were similar detachments throughout Britain supporting the divisions bracing themselves for invasion.

THE RAOC CHALLENGE

"'God, what a war!" he said. "There's always some blasted spare part missing and you can't get a sausage out of anybody urgently! It was different when we only had rifles.'" This complaint by a staff captain comes in J.K. Stanford's account of the Dunkirk evacuation and states the underlying problem with stark clarity.[3] The older depots were still organised largely as if they had 'only rifles', whereas they were trying to handle an ever increasing range of items. The requirements of an army of the 1940s were different, but they were nothing like as complex as they would become by 1945.

In June 1940 Bill Williams, now Director of Warlike Stores, and his fellow officers in the RAOC must have been faced with a confusion of powerful thoughts. The first must have been the immediate need to care for those exhausted troops who had made their way back from Dunkirk. The second, surely, concern for those who hadn't returned; to this would have been added later that June, the shock and anger at the sinking of the *Lancastria*. The human dimension came first, but there was also a harsh practical reality. The RAOC was already short of skilled, experienced men; now that position had worsened significantly.

Fast on the heels of the people would have come the materiel, the whole 1939 contents of Chilwell, those rows of gleaming bikes, utilities and lorries, all left behind, together with tons of ammunition and general stores. Utterly sickening. Third would have been the harsh lessons learnt in France about effective supply and efficient repair.

Among these thoughts must have been a driving desire to do something, anything. This would have slowly lost its intensity and been replaced, certainly in Bill's mind, by methodical, step-by-step planning of the route from A to B. The route? No one knew what, or how much, fighting would take place on the way, or indeed, with the serious threat of German invasion, whether they would even get to a starting point.

Some things were clear. If the British motor industry was going to produce the fighting materiel the army would need, the RAOC was to be the vital conduit between it and the troops. No one could have imagined the crazy number of different vehicles that would be produced over the following five years, but Bill must have assumed it would be many, for he set out to build a conduit – in effect, a massive motor distribution business, an RAOC organisation that could cope with the flood and create order out of it (with many a slip on the way). In Bill's obituary, written by his number two, twenty-five years later, John Hildreth wrote, 'many things went wrong in those early days, enough to daunt the spirit of a lesser man, but not Bill Williams'.[4]

An invasion on a massive scale would demand vehicles, armaments and equipment in an unprecedented number, but unlike the BEF, effectively supplied and supported. This would take time, and in the build-up effective storage would be needed. The existing ordnance depots dated back to before the Great War and so new space was needed, because the war of the mid-twentieth century would need supplies of a wholly different nature to past wars.

In the aftermath of Dunkirk, Winston Churchill writes in his account of the war that he contacted President Roosevelt, who immediately made US Ordnance reserves available – in reality, only a few old battleships.[5] Yet none of this came for free and the British Government had to part with its fast diminishing reserves of dollars and gold. This remained the case until Roosevelt achieved the passage of the Lend-Lease Act in March 1941.

The push to re-arm presented the RAOC with a store-man's nightmare. The separate UK motor companies each worked with great energy to manufacture their own models each with their own set of spare parts. Post Dunkirk, a great many vehicles were commandeered into service comprising an even greater variety of different makes and models.[6]

So, it wasn't just about volume, it was about hundreds of thousands of parts needed for all the different types which made up the volume. Official accounts talk about the tons of stores held or issued, and the picture conjured is of bails or crates of bulk. Truly, 'the devil is in the detail', which explains another of Bill's favoured sayings, 'a place for everything and everything in

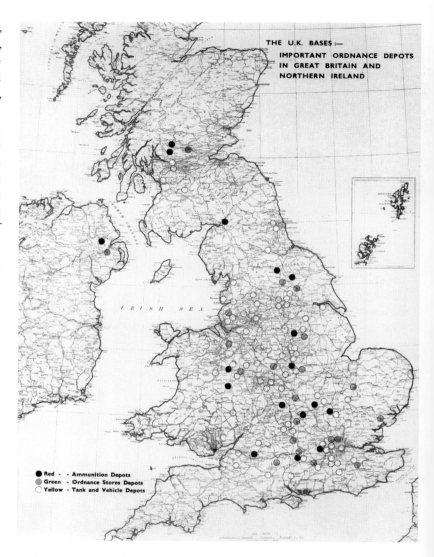

UK RAOC bases. (RLC Museum)

its place'. The task was to set up an organisation which could estimate what was needed, order it, receive it, check it, store it, find it, issue it and then maintain it.

THE POST-DUNKIRK PRIORITY

There was, however, a more immediate need, as Bill Williams recalled in a speech he made to a press conference in March 1942:[7]

Let me take you back to the days of June 1940. Every unit in the British Army, back from Dunkirk, turned to the RAOC and said, 'Give us new equipment'.

We had to reply: 'We have little to give'. How little most of you have probably guessed by now. Those few guns and other fighting stores which remained in Britain were in that old established and highly vulnerable depot Woolwich Arsenal. We knew this depot was an inevitable target for the enemy only a forty minutes flying time away.

The job had been scheduled to take several years in peace time, we did it in a few weeks, and created shadow depots in addition as an insurance against bombing attacks.

Construction of this vast new depot, which was to take the place of Woolwich Arsenal, had begun before the war, but in June 1940 only one shed was ready with others under erection, and the stores poured in as the roof went on and before the concrete floors were properly dried out.

Orders were immediately given for the work to be speeded; simultaneously orders were given to Woolwich to entrain all their most valuable stores and send a small portion of their staff. To this we added the flood of our new volunteer recruits and between them they tackled one of the most difficult problems of the war. The picture was a fantastic one. Every day for three weeks fifteen trainloads of all shapes and sizes of equipment left. Motor convoys carried additional loads.

At one time the railway company complained. Five hundred trucks had jammed the main line near the depot and had to be off loaded and cleared or the whole railway system of that part of Britain would have been paralysed.

Every officer, soldier and civilian available, from the Brigadier in command downwards, took off his jacket and finished the job in 48 hours. Whilst this was happening, great efforts were being made in our factories. The high production peaks of the Dunkirk period were being achieved. It would have been folly to send this new equipment to Woolwich Arsenal. They had therefore to come to our already overcrowded fields, now seas of mud.

Swarms of builders and contractors, hundreds of soldiers and a constant stream of trucks and railway trains carried on the business of both creating and operating what had become the largest ordnance depot in the world.

Donnington, in the Shropshire countryside, had been chosen by the War Office as the perfect site for the new depot, exactly the opposite of the depot it was to replace. There were problems: being located far enough away from vulnerable conurbations might mean safety from bombing, but it also meant being a good distance from the workforce. Hence the need for housing, but that would take time and time was one thing they didn't have. One result of the Dunkirk evacuation was that there was no shortage of troops in England and so sufficient numbers were soon drafted into Donnington, but to a life under canvas until Nissen huts could be erected, a low priority given the need to safely store what little there was that hadn't been left behind in France.[8]

Brigadier Charles de Wolff was made COO designate of the new depot, before being posted to France on mobilisation. He returned in May 1940.

SOME OF THE PEOPLE

De Wolff made a point of talking to the Woolwich staff early on so that they could be part of the process. This paid dividends with the number who chose to move to deepest Shropshire. He also saw the very obvious need for new housing and managed to persuade Wellington District Council to initially build 500 new houses with money made available by the Treasury.

Mary Wakely[9] moved to Donnington from Plumstead with her mother, older brother and her father, a veteran of the Great War who was a storeman at Woolwich. They moved into one of the first houses to be built. The very first boasted tile roofs and wooden floors, but with material shortages, the later houses had flat roofs and concrete floors and staircases. For Mary's family, being surrounded by green fields was not such a shock since they were used to Plumstead Common; the same was not true of those arriving from the East End, for whom the walk to school over fields was a shock. They, like all civilians in wartime, faced rationing; Mary vouched for the fact that they truly never saw a banana!

Sadly for all the newcomers from London, they were met with a certain amount of resentment from the locals, who were witnessing what they perhaps saw as the destruction of a beautiful rural scene by the massive depot, known to all as 'the dump', but also by three large, tented army camps. The depot did, however, bring more secure employment than that offered by the local iron works and mines; it also brought wealth to local businesses.

Mary's father continued to work as a storeman in the new depot until he died in 1945 from the lingering after-effects of the Great War. Her mother was one of many skilled packers whose role was vital in getting stores to the troops in good working order. Mary herself later worked in records office of the depot, handling the files of some 5,000 civilian staff.

At the top of Mary's road a number of houses were set aside for ATS girls, and Mary remembered them marching to the depot each day, sometimes led by the garrison band. After the war a number of houses were occupied by homeless families until they could be found more permanent homes. Another post-war memory was of huts, and later a whole new building, occupied by displaced persons from Poland, a number of whom married local girls and became active members of the community. The themes from this story are echoed in the hundreds of depots that sprang up around the UK.

Another former ATS[10] remembered soldiers marching to the depot each morning and in the winter, with daylight saving regulations, a soldier carrying a lamp in the front and another at the rear. On arriving at the depot she would be faced with typing in a shed with no heating, so that periodically they would be taken to a room with a fire to warm up.

Elsie Taylor, whose job it was to clean lenses on binoculars and telescopes, remembered the pleasure of being with so many young people and enjoying concerts and visits from famous entertainers including Workers' Playtime and the Squadronaires. This was another theme echoed elsewhere. Probably for the first time in our history, thousands of young people found themselves on campus with a focus on war work but with many of the same temptations and pleasures of twenty-first-century university life.

COD DONNINGTON AND THE ARMAMENTS DEPOTS

The depot was responsible for the storage and supply of all warlike stores for the army to all theatres of war – guns of all calibres, tracked self-propelled gun mountings including tanks, wireless, radar, and later, all supersonic equipment. By 1943 de Wolff was commanding 15,000 British troops, 3,200 ATS, some 2,000 Italian POWs and 3,000 civilians. Of this number there were some 4,000 clerks working together in one large building dealing with the issue of stores. Paperwork was transmitted by Lamson tubes, which some readers may remember from department stores of the 1950s. The site had seven buildings each covering 9 acres, all contained together with 7 miles of railway and two marshalling yards within a perimeter fence that extended to a distance of some 6½ miles. In time, the depot created some thirteen sub-depots scattered round the country from Yorkshire to Dorset and Somerset.[11]

On 22 June 1941 the German–Russian pact came to an end and Russia joined the war against Germany. Both Prime Minister Churchill and the Minister of Supply, Lord Beaverbrook, placed a high priority on making materiel available to the Russians, notwithstanding the relative insecurity of the British Isles. It follows that supplies to Russia were an important feature of the depot's work, as *John Bull*[12] magazine reported:

Ah, here was a man just back from Russia. He braved the Arctic seas and the German dive-bombers to take tanks to our Allies. With the thermometer at more than forty below freezing, our ordnance lads worked twenty-four hours a day to clear the ships before another convoy arrived. It was dawn at 10.30 a.m. and dusk at three – so they had to work with lights on even with 'Jerry' overhead. And men of the RAOC manned the light anti-aircraft guns.

And here was another man from Russia. He had gone to teach the Russians all about our tanks and the multitudinous spare parts accompanying them. 'Loveable' was his word for these people. They surrender their cold reserve slowly, and then become the friendliest people in the world.

Matilda tanks for Russia.

As one instance of the all-outness of Russia in the war effort, he said that women are being sent into the munition factories to work alongside their husbands. When they have learned the job themselves, their menfolk go into the army. Yet the one ambition of the women is to learn as quickly as possible, and of the men to teach them with all speed.

The National Motor Museum has an instruction manual for Churchill tanks written in Russian.

De Wolff, or 'Wolffy' as he was known, was obviously fond of story-telling. Donnington dealt with many of the supplies to Russia. Before shipment, everything had to undergo 'articisation' to enable it to operate at very low temperatures. The equipment and associated spare parts would then go by ship from Liverpool. The depot would pack everything and then, with sickening regularity, have to open all the packing cases for inspection by Russian delegates. Invariably this delayed matters and so the shipments missed the boat. Not a popular thing to do and matters escalated, with Wolffy being summoned to the War Office. Not one to be overawed, Wolffy suggested that the Russians post a man to Donnington. This, together with de Wolff's easy charm, solved the problem.[13] He was a colourful character. Bill had a photograph of him, a rather tall, distinguished, moustached man, but profoundly deaf with a Bakelite headphone connected to a leather-covered box that he carried under his arm.

The picture below shows him walking next to the Queen, with the King and Bill following behind. Wolffy had a lovely story about this visit. He tells of his friendship with Dr Woods, the Bishop of Lichfield, and how the bishop told him that the King and Queen were planning to visit Donnington. He took great delight in making all the arrangements, including a specially constructed 'ladies' for Her Majesty, well before Bill and the War Office received their formal notification.[14]

Donnington, along with other depots, later supplied the African campaign and here, 'articisation' was replaced by 'desertisation' of equipment. When guns were first sent to the desert, after a few miles they stopped as the tracks clogged with sand. The fitting of a relatively simple flange addressed the problem.

Donnington wasn't alone in supplying armaments and technical stores. Bob Hiam had come to the corps direct from Dunlop and was given the

Crusader tanks for Russia.

The Queen with Brigadier de Wolff at COD Donnington.

Colonel Hiam at a COO meeting.

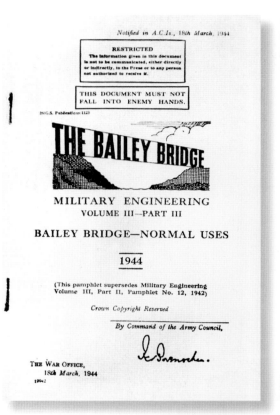

Bailey bridge manual, COD Old Dalby. (RLC Museum)

Bailey bridge in Italy. (RLC Museum)

job of creating a vehicle sub-depot for Chilwell at Old Dalby, a village nestling on the southern edge of the Vale of Belvoir. However, in 1940, when the demand for more armaments stores became acute, Old Dalby became a central ordnance depot. Its role was the storage and distribution of engineering and signals equipment, ranging from wireless sets to Bailey bridges; armaments including anti-tank guns and Bofors anti-aircraft guns; small arms and workshop machinery. Old Dalby was also responsible for kitting out ordnance mobile workshop lorries.[15] Bob Hiam later took his experience of armaments stores across with him after D-Day when he commanded the huge AOD, first in Normandy and later in Antwerp.[16]

Private John Frost[17] remembers a call being made for men with clerking experience. He volunteered and found himself posted to Old Dalby. He recalled a massive office with row after row of desks and paper, in Frost's own words, 'the army runs on paper'.

Working alongside Donnington and Old Dalby was COD Greenford, commanded first by Brigadier Johnson-Davis and then by Brigadier Goldstein on his return from Malta after the siege. Greenford's main functions were the receipt of warlike stores from manufacturers, their storage, maintenance and

The Queen with the ATS at COD Greenford.

Field gun at COD Greenford.

The Queen with Brigadier Goldstein at COD Greenford.

Gun barrels at COD Greenford.

Mobile guns at COD Greenford.

issue to units at home and overseas. The depot also assembled complete units from many thousands of single parts. As with the other depots, there were workshops working alongside.[18]

AMMUNITION DEPOTS

Ammunition storage was a major concern with the constant threat of bombing raids. Again, the War Office had thought ahead and had a team of Royal Engineers digging out 1 million tons of stone from deep under Corsham, near Bath, to create secure subterranean storage to take ammunition from the more vulnerable existing depot at Bramley.

Bramley, the oldest and most old-fashioned of the CADs, had been built by German prisoners of war in 1917–18 as a 'marrying' point for ammunition components.[19] It carried out all the normal functions, with a mix of sheds storing live ammunition, inert components and laboratories.

Of more immediate concern was the need to supply ammunition to counter the invasion that was expected in a matter of weeks. The existing depots were too remote and so a number of smaller depots were set up largely

in the open. The Royal Ordnance factories were running near capacity and storage was becoming a real challenge. More open air 'dumps' were set up, but this was not a long-term solution and so attention was turned first to accelerating Corsham and then to Longtown.[20]

The Monkton Farleigh mine, which was the largest of three that made up CAD Corsham, sat 100ft below grazing cattle overlooking the city of Bath. The mine extended to some 80 acres. The depot took seven years to build and some 7,000 sappers and contractors were involved in its construction. The tunnelling work, removing vast quantities of Bath stone, was meat and drink to the former coal miners employed on the work; that was, until July 1938 when the War Office insisted it should take its first delivery of ammunition. The depot was divided into ten sections separated by steel doors

Roadside ammunition storage post-Dunkirk. (RLC Museum)

and concrete walls. Just as one section was complete, the railway trucks, which had carried out the quarried stone, brought in live ammunition. The story is of very anxious miners and sappers clearing new tunnels while storemen transported ammunition on a rather precarious and noisy internal railway!

In time, the walls were painted white and the depot's own power station was built, as were barrack blocks to house the 350 soldiers and ATS who operated the depot.[21] N.J. McCamley's book, *Secret Underground Cities*, documents the building of Corsham, but also other installations for the RAF and navy. In relation to Corsham itself, McCamley tells of the dissatisfaction of the RAOC with the initial narrow-gauge railway and overhead rope system and of their delight when this was replaced by a state-of-the-art belt conveyor in 1942 which added greatly to both speed and health and safety.

Corsham was, by any standards, a triumph of engineering. There were miles of bright white tunnels, home to conveyor belts transporting tons of ammunition from their storage areas to the 1¼-mile tunnel that led to the Great Western Railway line, which took the dangerous load to its destination. Construction and operation were beset with challenges: rock falls, the sudden change from Bath stone to wet gravel and the humidity which eventually necessitated air conditioning. The creation of this massive underground ammunition store was top secret, so McCamley is justified in his amusement at finding this entry in the diary of Miss Berrett, a young Trowbridge school teacher: 'Wed, August 27th – Went to Corsham and saw men at work on the munitions dump which stretches underground for a great distance.'

The surface CADs also benefitted from mechanisation. Longtown, in the West Riding, had been an ordnance factory in the Great War but had been left to become derelict. In January 1939 construction of a new depot began on the site. Progress was painfully slow until a telegram announced the imminent arrival of 4,000 tons of cordite – this concentrated the mind.

At the end of August 1939, the depot staff had comprised two officers, one warrant officer (the chief clerk) and six civilians, and the transport consisted of six wheelbarrows. By 4 September, 200 militia had been drafted in and four Scammell Mechanical Horses hired from LNE Railway. Longtown Central Ammunition Depot was declared open. It later expanded to store 60,000 tons of ammunition in some 252 magazines. Longtown offers yet another example of the conundrum faced by the RAOC: do you place your depots near to a plentiful supply of labour, or away from people to minimise the risk to life from accidents or enemy bombing? Longtown was surrounded by farmland and so it was very difficult to find staff with the right experience. The problem was solved by the provision of free travel from neighbouring towns.[22]

The need for yet further depots soon became clear. Nesscliff,[23] a site near Shrewsbury, was identified and building by the Ministry of Supply began in early 1941 and was completed some three years later. Like other ammunition depots it was principally served by railway, both for the receipt of ammunition from Royal Ordnance factories and its issue to divisions or docks for transport overseas. Again like other depots, it had a large repair shop where returned ammunition could be inspected and made serviceable.

The last of the 'big five' ammunition depots was built in the period of the latter part of the Desert War at Kineton, a village between Warwick and Banbury. The author of the RAOC official history notes that it was built by military labour in under two years, which compared favourably with the time that it took the Ministry of Supply to build Nesscliff. Kineton is now the principal CAD for the Royal Logistics Corps.

The competitive tone was probably inevitable given the very close relationship between the RAOC and the Ministry through which major contracts with suppliers were made. That the relationship was cordial as well as competitive is clear from the letter Bill Williams received from an opposite number at the Ministry when he was awarded a knighthood in 1946:

> The most noisy and hilarious congratulations on your KBE. Whether this award has been given to you for your work in Ordnance or as Chief Publicity Officer of the Army I do not know … when in Washington I saw nothing but your dhobie mark in every General's room.

That, though, is for later in the story …

WHAT THE DEPOTS DID

An ordnance depot must have been like a vast distribution warehouse, but without computers. Delivery wouldn't be by a courier who would leave a card if the customer was out, it was by soldiers, often under fire and always under pressure. I will leave it again to Bill Williams[24] to add flesh to the bare bones of the question regarding what a depot actually did:

> The fighting and technical equipment of the British Army consists of half a million different bits and pieces. These are made by many hundreds of different manufacturers scattered all over this country and overseas. The maker of a wireless set, for example, does not make the valves which go with it, or the batteries which work it. The maker of a gun does not make

the carriage on which it moves, or the sights and the hundred and one intricate items of technical equipment, without which it cannot be fired. Somewhere the incomplete equipment has to be brought together.

Even the tanks come to us with empty hulls into which we fit the armament, the wireless and the vast array of fighting and technical equipment before they can be issued as fighting tanks.

A 25-pdr. gun is only a headline to newspapers. To a Central Ordnance Depot it is 2,000 different pieces, plus another hundred accessories. If any of these accessories are missing, if one maker falls behind in his production programme, if one case is packed for Libya and an essential part left out, this 25-pdr. gun cannot be used.

A key role for the RAOC was to estimate the likely requirement for both original equipment and spare parts. This would depend on wear and tear but also on estimated casualties from enemy action. With motor vehicles in particular this must have been virtually impossible. Bill continued, for his press conference audience:

You can see there the orders coming in from the War Office, the formations and the overseas theatres of war. We use teleprinters for speed and accuracy. You can see the tanks, the guns, the packing cases leaving the depots for Libya and Russia and India and even America. Codes and symbols tell the initiated their destination, and ensure that the right packages are loaded on the right ship.

Let us suppose that certain packages of vital accessories for a shipload of guns are loaded in another ship, and that particular ship in the convoy is sunk. It means that the guns will be useless when they arrive in the theatre of war.

You can see women and men whose job it is to keep an accurate record of all the bits and pieces they deal with. You can see others undergoing their infantry training for defence of the depots and for service overseas. You can see tanks being tested and fitted for service. You can see repairs carried out. Ordnance depots are towns in themselves, humming with activity alive for twenty-four hours every day.

Had you tuned into the BBC Home Service at 7 or 8 a.m. on Saturday, 19 July 1941, you might have heard a slightly different story in a recorded piece by Richard Sharp[25] about his visit to an army supply depot. It was the very old story of the Crimea and how an army supply depot managed to send a shipment consisting entirely of left boots. Sharp makes the valid point

that with a twentieth-century depot handling some 97,000 different items, the potential for mistakes is increased exponentially. Sharp marvelled at how the new depot was equipped: its own electricity plant, telephone exchange, furnaces and print works, but then said this:

All this is very nice and comforting, of course. It's good to know that we have all this stuff, particularly when you remember that it's only passing through, a sample of what thousands of factories are pouring in to be distributed to the troops, but – the depot that issued that shipload of left boots was a big place too, no doubt. What about the efficiency of this place? The printing press prints two million pieces of paper a week. Think what muddles you could make with two million pieces of paper?

The answer came from a lieutenant colonel in charge of organisation and planning, one of the 'industry types' that Stanford disliked so much. This officer's approach was simple: bring to bear the skills learnt from industry. Things such as planning routes so that lorries both go out from the depot full but also return full. The lorries covered 1¼ million miles in three months and so the savings in petrol alone would have been huge. It was not just petrol; rubber was in short supply and so all road journeys had to count. And not just with transport; the way transactions were routed through the depot made a huge difference to staffing requirements. The lieutenant colonel estimated that better procedures had saved 55 per cent in costs. As the war entered its fourth and fifth year this would matter, not so much because of money but, because there was simply not the people available, labour saving became very much the order of the day.

THE MOTOR VEHICLE DEPOTS

The War Office invited the press to a further visit to Chilwell in March 1940 and what comes though even more clearly from the press reports is the military strength that the depot then boasted. We should bear in mind that in March 1940 there was a clear expectation of the British Expeditionary Force returning home victorious. The *Nottingham Journal*[26] noted the growth of the depot since their last visit. Now it held some 140,000 different spare parts. They set this in context by observing that a motor manufacturer would only have around 20,000. They had this to say, possibly for consumption by the German intelligence service:

AMONG THE MEN WHO MAKE THE ARMY'S WHEELS GO ROUND

Lumbering Cruiser Tanks rushed by with a noise like a London tube railway, tank engines swinging across huge workshops by the aid of travelling cranes …

The final instalment of the visit was to the air raid shelter capable of holding thousands of soldiers and civilians.

'You are now underneath the wood you saw beyond our boundaries,' said an officer guide. 'Over your head are a hundred feet of solid rock and earth. No bomb can harm you here.'

The Cruiser tanks were those manufactured by Nuffield Mechanisation and they played a small but important role in defending the forces retreating to Dunkirk. They would come into their own in the desert.

The other message this time was the significance of the depot as a local employer. The report was of thousands of people working there, including the largest concentration of ATS in the country, some 600 women carrying out a wide range of duties including delivering lorries across the country:

There are no windscreens on the lorries destined for active service and the driving of these vehicles during the abnormal weather that prevailed early this year was a test of real endurance from which these girls emerged with flying colours.

ATS women would become a vital feature of all ordnance depots, taking on roles from cooks to drivers and mechanics, not forgetting sitting side-by-side with civilians in clerical and warehousing work.

It wasn't just women drivers, civilian John Perkins[27] recalled the bitterly cold journeys all around the country delivering vehicles, 'During the time they didn't have glass in the windscreens during the war, in order to keep warm I covered my chest in grease under cardboard and newspaper'. John had begun working as a non-established driver at Chilwell in 1940, having previously been employed on-site while working for a civilian contractor. As he managed to find his way around the country, he found his lack of reading and writing skills something of an advantage when all the signposts had been removed! He regularly led convoys because of his keen sense of direction.

During the long London Blitz convoys were regularly stuck in lines of trucks just sitting there waiting for the bombs to drop. John's biggest scare was not from the Luftwaffe but from one of his fellow drivers. They were bringing large flat-back American Diamond T transporters from Glasgow

Docks into England via Carlisle and Shap Summit. The front truck had one on the back and one on tow. The driver of the rear vehicle was supposed to use his brakes to help control the descent, but did not! The trio of Diamond Ts ran away down the old A66 for miles and miles, brakes smoking.

On 28 October 1940, the *Nottingham Guardian*[28] reported on the influence that business methods brought to bear at Chilwell. The issue was the old chestnut: the right part, in the right place, at the right time. The example given was of a lorry in the desert breaking a spring but being back in the field in full working order a matter of hours later. It was not just any spring, it had to be the right spring – the right make and the right model. It all came down to census records. Chilwell recorded every vehicle in the army, which unit was using it and where, on a hi-tech card system. The article describes in great detail how a system of punch holes and partial holes (a 'long skewer or fat knitting needle set in a wooden handle like a bradawl') could be used to locate individual vehicles. This information would then inform the depots shipping spare parts to the workshops supporting the relevant units. The article continued:

The office work is on a scale that has to be seen to be believed. Soldiers and civilians, girls in and out of uniform, unerringly record the comings and goings of things they have never seen – and might not recognised if they saw them – to and from places they have never been to and in some cases have never heard of … this though is the lesser part of the job, the rest is to place those right things just where they will be wanted by the Army everywhere. It is useless to have Ford back axles in a Maltese workshop if a Morris wants a new front axle. The spare parts must be constantly related to the particular vehicles that are in use in a particular area.

Chilwell was up and running, first under the command of Brigadier Whitaker, who succeeded Bill, and then under Brigadier Readman. 'Reddy' had been a Reservist while pursuing a career in industry. The former had given him a familiarity with the corps and its ways, the latter had provided access to modern management. If, under Bill, Chilwell had been conceived and born, under Reddy it was moulded into the vital part of the Allies' war machine that it would become. Reddy went on to be promoted to major general and then returned to industry, retiring as managing director of English Steel Corporation Tool Co., Manchester, in 1958.

The largest space at Chilwell[29], Shed 157, had been used in early 1940 to house 2,800 troops while barracks were being built. It then provided shelter for 7,000 Dunkirk evacuees. Notwithstanding these numbers, Brigadier

Above: COD Chilwell, artist's impression. (RLC Museum)

Right: The Queen with civilian packers at COD Chilwell.

Readman foresaw manpower shortages as the depot grew and more men were called up. Shed 157 therefore became the home for 'detail stores' – many numbers of small items. A power-operated wooden slat conveyor was installed to run along three-quarters of the length of the building and, in turn, this fed four conveyor belts. These carried stores from receipt to the correct bin and then from the relevant section to emerge as packed requisitions. The method of storage and the recording of stores became standardised across all depots using the system introduced at Chilwell. It is estimated that by the end of the war 13 million cartons containing 300 million items were packed by Chilwell people.

Chilwell's store of vehicles and spares swelled and so the need for sub-depots became apparent. Buildings ranging from soap works, shoe factories, blanket mills, chain store restaurants and even hunt kennels were requisitioned and represented some forty sub-depots controlling some 200 premises, in total 6 million sq. ft of covered space and 2 million sq. ft of open storage. The depots were receiving all of the army's tyres and inner tubes, all the tank tracks, wheels and wheel assemblies, all the anti-mining devices, vehicle engines, rear axles, gearboxes, cylinder blocks and radiators, as well as a multitude of smaller items, from manufacturers. A vast open store for complete vehicles was located at West Hallam near Derby.

Central Ordnance Depot Derby, in Sinfin Lane near to where engineers in the neighbouring Rolls-Royce factory hand-built Merlin engines, was created as a major sub-depot to Chilwell by 'Robby' Robinson, a former managing director at Dunlop. He brought with him experience of man management. Among other initiatives, in 1943 he instituted the production of a daily news-sheet for the depot, which itself tells the story of the lengths to which Robby went in order to build a team.

Civilian workers at COD Chilwell.

Bedford OXD vehicles delivered at COD Chilwell. (© Vauxhall Heritage Archive)

Good storekeeping at COD Derby. (RLC Museum)

The news-sheet[30] gave news of the war (for example, Operation Market Garden and the Arnhem mission), day by day without any hype and not hiding the terrible losses. At a more parochial level, an earlier edition had a piece about gaskets and how they had to be handled carefully, and later there is a piece telling how, in view of shortages, some gaskets were being made from wrapping paper. On the subject of paper, a new recruit was quoted as asking why there was so much paperwork – the answer, 'it's all about checking; if everyone took more care it wouldn't be needed!' The entertainments section picked up on the popularity of film and of big band music for dances. Interestingly, there were also discussion groups – on 20 October 1943, one on science and religion.

At Derby, like most of the depots, both training and education were provided to all staff including motor engineering, building trades, gardening, poultry keeping, accountancy and shorthand, languages, history, politics and science.

THE USA

A major role for all depots was the receipt of supplies from the United States under the provisions of the Lend-Lease Act. In September 1941, the head of US Ordnance, Major General Wesson, made a brief visit. This was followed a year later by a far more extensive visit by his successor, Major General Lewin Campbell. He visited Chilwell and then Old Dalby on 5 November 1942. In the booklet on Chilwell produced for his visit, its pivotal role was made clear:

Chilwell is the Army Centre of Mechanisation … it is the base that supplies vehicles, assemblies and spare parts to the whole of our troops in this country, to our overseas Forces in all parts of the Empire, and to our allies – among whom the Russians have been receiving a steady flow of supplies.[31]

Bill Williams praised Campbell for all the efforts made by US Ordnance in providing the stream of guns, tanks and vehicles for the African front line. When explaining how they did it, Campbell put the question:

How do you eat an elephant? When you can do that, you will know how American Ordnance tackled the job. You cut it up into little pieces and get through it that way. The big word is decentralise. You distribute it around your depots. You then hand it round to your officers, who then break it down into a little job of vital work for every one of their staffs.[32]

The relationship with US Ordnance and manufacturers would move to centre stage in the preparations for D-Day.

THE ROLE OF WOMEN

The role of women was massively important, as was apparent from an article in the fortnightly publication by the Army Bureau on Current Affairs entitled 'The Women Bogey'. This sought to bolster the argument in favour of women retaining the more prominent position in the workplace that they had enjoyed during hostilities after the war. Newspaper articles appeared regularly emphasising the crucial importance of the work women undertook in the ordnance depots, to say nothing of Royal Ordnance factories, manufacturing companies and indeed just about every walk of life.

On 15 June 1942, the *Yorkshire Evening Post*[33] reported on the role of the ATS at Chilwell, which had the largest such unit in the country. The chief of the ATS stressed that 'it has never been the aim of the ATS to turn girls into mere weak imitations of men. Girls are individualists and throughout the organisation there must be the individualistic touch'. The article highlighted the range of tasks undertaken: machine shop, drawing offices, stores and, of course, the fourteen cookhouses that kept the depot operating twenty-four hours a day:

More specifically women undertake the Articisation of tanks bound for Russia and the Desertisation of those bound for Africa and the East. To counter the effects of condensation in tanks being delivered to hot climates, a ball of lime is suspended inside. All parts are 'sozzled' with oil and grease.

Not surprisingly, the article finds ATS women who in their former lives were in the public eye, such as the first woman to cross the desert on a motorcycle and who later competed against men in army trials. No wonder men were scared!

A similar theme emerges from the *Sunday Times*, on 1 November 1942,[34] of a visit to 'Woolwich-in-the-country', described as being in the north but more probably Donnington in Shropshire. The special correspondent tells how, 'in that radiant summer of 1940 when the sunshine seemed to mock our anxieties as France tottered to capitulation', he visited a 'new Woolwich buried in the countryside many miles from London'. He marvelled at the size of the place but also the many innovations that had been introduced, adding, 'the American authorities were so impressed by "Woolwich-in-the-country"

ATS personnel leaving RAOC Hilsea.

that they sent an Ordnance expert across by bomber to study its methods'. In relation to women he wrote:

> There are girls wherever you turn and most of them are in the ATS … in one of the huts in the training section a slim 18 year old ATS corporal was lecturing officers, soldiers and ATS on the identification of wireless components … later in the instrument repair shop a good looking young woman with sergeants stripes pinned on her overalls paused for a moment from measuring thousandths of an inch to talk rather diffidently about her civilian studies at five British and foreign universities and to admit that she was a BSc Edin (First Class Hons) … in terms of facilities he saw the hall with a loan collection from the National Gallery on show.

The work of the ATS prompted an exchange that paints a contrasting picture of the time.[35] Early in the war, Dame Helen Gwynne Vaughan was the officer commanding the ATS at the War Office. Betty Perks' diary tells that she was a 'real old battle-axe' with definite ideas about women and their role in the services. Many of the younger ATS girls at Chilwell pleaded to be allowed to wear trousers while driving army vehicles, firstly because they were warmest and secondly because it was very difficult to sit in an army vehicle in a tight skirt without showing 'everything!' Dame Helen wouldn't hear of it – she was horrified that her young ladies would even suggest such thing. A cartoon of an ATS girl climbing into a lorry revealing frilly knickers changed her mind.

The idea of joining the ATS and working with the RAOC was not always attractive at first sight. Margaret Sherman, for one, was not at first inspired:

We were given our posting instructions and gathered round with excitement. A lot of us had hopefully asked for London District or South Eastern Command. Would we get it? Mary and I heard with a good deal of dismay that we were going to a Central Ordnance Depot somewhere in Northern England.

'Perhaps it won't be for longer than the initial three months,' Mary said comfortingly. 'Ordnance, who'd want that?' I said with the nightmare vision of millions of issue and receipt vouchers. I didn't know then that the only thing I'd hate about Ordnance would be leaving it.[36]

The ATS did change lives. Gwendoline Walker joined up in 1942 and after initial training had to sit an intelligence test. She was summoned by the senior ATS officer at COD Derby and asked what job she wanted to do. She replied that she had thought of becoming a cook. Her grandparents had been in service and this was the life she had expected to lead. She had left her job in a shop and without telling her parents had 'escaped' to join up. She remembered the shock at the officer telling her that she had a high IQ and could do anything she wanted. She had no idea what an IQ was, but suggested that she might work in stores. She went from Derby to Greenford and was a very effective storewoman before moving toward clerical work and accounting after the war, 'The ATS was where I found myself'.[37]

SMALL ARMS

With the presence of barracks and drill halls in many UK towns, it is perhaps not surprising that there were also former ordnance depots in many parts of the country. Near Northampton, for example, there had been barracks and powder magazines at Weedon since 1803. The records show that in 1808 the following announcement appeared in the *National Register*: 'We learn from undoubted authority that the Government is about to establish an Ordnance Depot at Weedon in Northamptonshire of extra-ordinary magnitude and importance.'[38]

The central location in the country was a particular attraction. In the Second World War, Weedon became the centre for the supply of small arms and machine guns to the whole army, at home and abroad. Weedon worked with its fellow central ordnance depot at Old Dalby in Leicestershire and locally with sub-depots at Northampton, Long Buckby and Heyford.

QUARTERMASTER'S STORES

The general stores depots had eaten up manpower with the need to handle heavy and bulky items. Mechanisation through the use of Lister trucks, mechanical horses and forklifts made a massive difference in terms of efficiency of operation.

The Didcot site, now the Didcot power stations, had been selected as suitable for a depot as far back as 1915, when it was recognised as being particularly well placed for rail access. During the First World War, Didcot[39] supplied those quartermaster's stores that Woolwich couldn't handle, items such as hospital and camp furniture and barrack stores. Didcot's rural location did, however, present problems with staffing. This was eased by an approach to Oxford University for volunteers from its OTC; members of the Eton OTC also volunteered help in 1916. An observer in the 1920s noted 'the monstrous size of the place. It is so big it seems unreal'. The depot was a series of iron corrugated or wooden sheds linked by railway lines. The latter presented a major problem: there was little, if any, road access. In due course this was successfully addressed.

In the mid-1930s there had been a workforce at Didcot of 150 military and 1,500 civilian employees. A further 900 were added with the transfer of the clothing depot from Pimlico. Hitherto the army had manufactured its own uniforms, many at the Pimlico premises. As the prospect of war

Weedon Barracks, Northamptonshire.

COD Weedon. (RLC Museum)

increased, the War Office saw the value in the vast Didcot site for bulky stores and clothing was moved once more, this time to the former pickle factory at Branston near Burton-on-Trent. A new 650,000 sq. ft heated shed was constructed on the Didcot site, three sheds were taken over at Longtown, (on the same site as CAD Longtown) and sub-depots set up at Basing (on the same site as CAD Bramley), Elstree, Olympia and Boughton.

Another sub-depot, Regional Depot RAOC Thatcham,[40] was set up in 1940. Tragically the new commanding officer, Lieutenant Colonel V.H. Urquart, was killed by enemy bombing on 16 August 1940. In 1942 the whole depot was handed over to the Americans, who created there the biggest US Army European depot with sites at Thatcham, Greenham Common, Newbury Racecourse and Hermitage. The depot had a vital role in supporting D-Day and subsequent operations in north-west Europe.

The range of stores held by Didcot and its sub-depots was huge and included equipment for mountain and snow warfare, airborne equipment and assault, commando and jungle warfare, in addition to bicycles, industrial gases, camouflage equipment, camp equipment and household utensils. In terms of numbers, there were 7,410 personnel in 1943, comprising 1,150 RAOC, 1,000 Royal Pioneer Corps, 850 ATS and 4,410 civilians. Annual expenditure rose from £3 million in 1939 to £75 million in 1945, with the annual tonnage shipped increasing from 18,000 tons to 1.5 million tons over the same period.

With the shortage of civilian staff at Didcot a system of outstation working was developed, where particularly married women could carry out tasks closer to their homes. A similar set-up was used at Chilwell and other depots.

A BRAND NEW MULTI-PURPOSE DEPOT FOR D-DAY

In late 1940 it became clear that there was still insufficient capacity in the RAOC depots. Accordingly a brand new depot[41] was to be set up under the command of Brigadier Palmer. This depot was going to break the mould by bringing together all warlike stores including, importantly, motor transport, which by then had taken centre stage.

Photographs of Palmer show him always with a pipe, a small man with neatly combed hair. He had been on that first ordnance officer's course but, it seems, had not covered himself with glory having failed the ammunition exam paper. He had commanded 1 BOD in the British Expeditionary Force. We don't know whether he sailed on the *Lancastria*, but it is certain that many of those men who lost their lives had been under his command.

Brigadier Palmer at COO meeting.

On 13 January 1941 Bill Williams wrote to him with the instructions to build a very large and entirely new type of depot as a key platform for the invasion of mainland Europe. Palmer would go on to be promoted to the rank of major general with oversight of all the motor transport within the corps.

Palmer was a man with twenty-nine years of experience in ordnance and he set to his task with relish at having the rare opportunity of fitting buildings to stores rather than, as had been more usual, fitting stores into buildings that had been built for other purposes. The depot was to be different in two other important ways. In view of the difficulty in securing sufficient local civilian staff, it was to be an all military establishment. It was also to deal with every kind of supply except for ammunition, and it was to have the largest tank repair shop in the country.[42]

In having the opportunity to design the buildings, much thought was given to optimum size. Large buildings of 300,000 to 400,000 sq. ft, such as those at Chilwell or Donnington, were thought too generous a target for air attack, whereas the smaller 40,000 sq. ft buildings favoured by the RAF were too small to be operated with maximum staff efficiency. A happy medium of 100,000 sq. ft was selected and worked well. There were to be other 'special' features: walls and roofs were to be independently supported; concrete roofs provided protection from incendiary attack; rail and road routes inside sheds helped to avoid double handling, and having them sunk meant that ramps could be dispensed with. The floors of the sheds would be on a slight gradient sloping down from the 'receipts' end to the 'issues' section. Clerical functions were also decentralised to improve liaison between 'stores' and 'paper'. The covered space totalled 3.75 million sq. ft.

The site was to be chosen from Towcester, Warwick, Cheltenham, Swindon, Oxford and Aylesbury, which allowed proximity to a civilian workforce in peacetime and the avoidance of airfields. The place chosen was Bicester, just outside Oxford, where today thousands flock to shop and which is to become a garden city – then it was countryside, which those fighting sought to preserve as English.

I rather think that the Bicester project was very special for Bill, not only because of its clear strategic importance but also because it in some way retraced the steps that created Chilwell. Bill had spoken of the frequent visits to the embryonic Chilwell by his boss, Lionel Hoare. It is clear that Bill, too, made frequent visits to Bicester.

Cecil Pinchin,[43] of Bicester, remembers as a young boy Bill lodging in their terraced house. It was a place where he could escape. He lodged alongside two young RAF men, whom Cecil remembers were somewhat in awe of him. The three lodged with Cecil's mother; Cecil's father was away each night manning the fire station. Cecil told me of 'this big man with flat hat and shiny boots' carrying him around on his shoulders. There is a road in C section of Bicester Depot named Williams Way. Bill had another connection with Oxfordshire: up to the end of the eighteenth century, the Williams family had been fellmongers in the village of Wheatley, a little to the south of Bicester.

STORAGE AND RECORD-KEEPING

One of the many lessons brought home from the BEF was that the huge variety of different practices operated by the different depots led to chaos in the field. Didcot had experimented with mechanical record-keeping on NCR machines. Chilwell was committed to the manual Visidex system since it could be used anywhere, whether in a huge home depot or in a field depot under fire. The decision was taken to standardise all depots on Visidex. It is apparent, though, from the depots' war diaries that there was resistance to this,

which often showed itself in blatant disregard. It was a constant battle, but one that Bill Williams eventually won.

Behind the Visidex record was a system for issues run by the control office of each depot. Indents for stores would be received from units and the stock record immediately updated for the items to be issued; those in stock would be issued straight away and the remainder entered on a 'dues out control' until the next receipt from suppliers.

Alongside record-keeping there was the question of physical storage. It seems that, at the beginning of the war, the standard storage box for just about everything was the disused ammunition case. The new influx of men from industry brought with them the latest techniques to maximise the use of space, to minimise damage in handling and to facilitate speedy identification for issues. Steel racking was introduced and over the years of the war packaging was refined and improved.

MANAGEMENT CHALLENGES

The presence in all the depots of men direct from industry with technical expertise in aspects of logistics posed management problems when they were put with men who had served in the BEF, some of whom had built up resentment for having their field promotions 'forgotten'. The direct entrants would be promoted to management positions and have to command (or try to command) troops who were, in effect, their workforce. That this was a live issue is clear from Bill Williams' 1942 speech:

To some of these men we gave direct commissions – just as the other branches of the army, such as the Engineers, the Medical Corps, also gave direct commissions. We gave these commissions for two reasons. Firstly, we were desperately short of officers. We had to have men who could carry the load at once, whilst others went through the ranks and were trained. Secondly, we wanted new blood and new experience as soon as possible. We wanted to get on with the job.

We have been criticised for opening the door to people who received direct commissions. How else would you have tackled the problem?

It required a great deal of effort on the part of senior officers to create an effective unit staffed in this way. It is interesting to read about the issue from two points of view. de Wolff was very much at the sharp end as COO trying to draw it all together. Stanford came from the regimental background, with an understandable loyalty to his soldiers. He tells how the whole thing came to a head when a contingent of 350 privates who had previously been managers in chain stores reported for duty:

> Their Managing Director had dug himself into the War Office and was now a field officer with one month's service. Their wives had driven to the camp in expensive limousines and parked them around the parade ground while they searched for billets … The mutterings among ex-corporals back from France became a steady rumble, especially when one private, with a foreign name, announced incautiously that he expected to be a sergeant in three days' time.

It seems that Woolfy heard about this and phoned Stanford to ask whether a certain Private X, who deals with millions of pounds of packing for Fuchs and Bieber, had arrived. This man was found and his skills put to good use, nevertheless good management was needed to integrate these skilled men into an army.

De Wolff had been invited to visit British businesses to get advice and ideas on setting up Donnington. It was to have the best possible chance of efficiency. Even in de Wolff's advice, though, it is possible to detect a hint of disapproval at this new way of doing things, what Stanford refers to as the 'New Army whose performance is bolstered by buns and cigarettes' (one assumes as opposed to old-fashioned army discipline):

> There were many 'experts' in civil life who, in civil life, were given Commissions, but they were just 'civilians' in uniform. Those who were posted to the War Office did not know the difference between standing to attention and standing at ease! One of these 'experts' was given the rank of Captain at the War office and six months later he was promoted to Major. He was a bachelor and lived in rooms in London. He had nothing to do when his duties ceased for the day and so he haunted all the night clubs and made himself a nuisance. This came to the ears of the QMG who told my General, 'I am demoting that officer to Captain. Send him to de Wolff and let him have go at him.'

It seems that this was thoroughly successful, as the officer emerged eighteen months later as a lieutenant colonel described as 'first class'. De Wolff applied his discipline to a number of such officers with equal success.[44]

Howard Palmer[45] had served in the Royal Artillery in the Great War. During the Second World War he became garrison officer at Donnington

with responsibility also for its twenty-eight sub-depots around the country. We would today describe his duties as 'facilities management'; indeed, he saw Donnington as a huge industrial concern consuming 200 tons of fuel in its power station each week.

Palmer offered a particular view on the conflict felt by ordnance officers between their 'professional' duties and soldiering:

> There must always be some conflict of interest, when Ordnance personnel can rightly claim to be fully occupied and usefully so on duties in which regimental fiddle-faddle is nothing but disruptive. The two just do not mix in the base organisations, and such training and skills as are required of all as soldiers and refreshers should be on the lines of the territorials, say, in a time and place of their own. I would go further and say that all Ordnance personnel should be able as soldiers to row and sail a boat, fly and jump from an aircraft, drive anything, climb a minor rock face, get over water and swim if he falls, pass a commando obstacle course, handle small arms efficiently, march and drill before he takes up his pen, file and phone. And I haven't mentioned fighting fires, resisting gas and giving first aid with a bit of rescue for luck.

It is clear, from his account of his time at the RAOC training centre at Leicester, that none of this was said tongue-in-cheek – soldiering was a serious business.

Just as big a management challenge was the meshing of military and civilian staff, again taking Bill Williams' own words:

> The staff of our great depots consists of a mixture of civilians, soldiers, and ATS. The principle we work on is to employ the right number of suitable civilians, plus sufficient soldiers to defend the depot in the event of invasion – (you must bear in mind that some of our depots are of more importance than aerodromes and must be defended) – and to provide a constant flow of trained men to the overseas theatres of war to create and man the base depots, advance depots and units in the field required to supply the modern armies with the vast range of weapons, tanks and other technical equipment.
>
> In the home depots civilians, soldiers and ATS are inter-mixed in every branch to ensure that soldiers get a proper training in the work they will have to do overseas and that when they are posted away there are civilians of sufficient skills to provide the necessary continuity and background to train new recruits.

A challenge for the RAOC, but also for the army as a whole, was the identification of people's skills and aptitudes, as Bill explains:

> One of the chief reasons for the successful organisation of our great depots is the appointment of Staff Controllers whose sole job in life is the fitting of round pegs into round holes. The system is a perfectly simple one, it consists of a personal interview by the Staff Controller of every civilian employee, A.T.S. or soldier, to find out the work on which they were employed in civil life, the name of the firm, the salary they earned, their hobbies, in fact anything which would help us to place that particular body in the job where he or she can give the best contribution to winning the war.

Bill made this point in his speech of March 1942. The previous winter, a committee under the chairmanship of Sir William Beveridge had studied the issue of the acute shortage of skilled mechanical and electrical tradesmen, with the remit to make better use of the army's technical skills. The Beveridge Committee[46] reported that skilled men were to be found in every part of the army with their skills largely unused and that, in particular, vehicle repair workshops were run by each of the RAOC, RASC and Royal Engineers, adding that those of the RAOC were the most efficient.

The committee recommended:

> Men should be enlisted not for this or that Corps, but into the Army as a single Service. On being received, examined and sorted at centres common to the whole Army, they should be posted from those centres to a definite Corps only when it is clear that they fit the requirements of those Corps and that any scarce skill posed by them will be turned to full account.

This focus on the best use of skills resulted in some 50,000 men being combed out of the army and returned to industry where their skills were most needed.

The committee's recommendation ran into the sand, with stiff opposition from regiments who did not want the morale of their men disturbed by moving key officers. I can't help thinking that there were a number of thorny issues about the relationship between the RAOC and other parts of the army. A point already mentioned was that the RAOC men were classed as non-combatant. This changed in October 1941 when the RAOC was accorded combatant status. The following passage from the speech is possibly a result:

Certain criticisms have been made on the employment of large numbers of soldiers in these depots, but now that I have given you the picture, I am sure you will agree that we must have soldiers passing through these depots, (incidentally the turnover is well over 100% per annum), to be trained for overseas and to provide a fighting force to defend these depots in an invasion.

The fact that we are now responsible for our own defence has of course released many thousands of Infantry for other purposes.

The committee went on to recommend the establishment in the Army of a Corps of Mechanical Engineers. It referred readers to the success of the Navy's use of mechanical engineers, adding that whilst the Navy's problems may be simpler it took specialisms seriously, quoting those for torpedoes, ordnance and electricity. It said:

> The Navy is machine minded. The Army cannot afford to be less so. The Navy sets engineers to catch, test, train and use engineers. Until the Army gives to mechanical and electrical engineers, as distinct from civil engineers, their appropriate place and influence in the Army system, such engineers are not likely to be caught, tested and trained as well as in the Navy; there is a danger that they will be missed by men whose main interests and duties lie in other fields.

This must have created quite a stir. The Beveridge Committee's recommendations were approved by the Army Council and a second committee was charged with implementation. This committee's members included Lieutenant General Ronald Weeks, Deputy Chief of the Imperial General Staff; Sir Robert Sinclair, Director of Army Requirements, who would go on to become chairman of Imperial Tobacco; and Mr A. W. Dunkley, director of the Anglo-Iranian Oil Company and a member of the Petroleum Board. They proposed that the technical elements of these three corps should be combined in the newly formed REME, which in future would carry out all major repair work. The RAOC would take over all vehicle and spare part provision. The RASC would focus on its transporting activities, since, at the same time, it lost it catering activities to the newly formed Army Catering Corps.

Towards the end of 1940 a standing committee on army administration had recommended the appointment of a Director General of Army Equipment, recognising the phenomenal growth in the number and variety of vehicles and other kinds of equipment. Lieutenant General Weeks was appointed, bringing experience from a career with Pilkington's as well as service in the Great War and in the Territorial Army between the wars. The formation of REME was probably a natural progression. Ronald Weeks would go on to become chairman of Vickers-Armstrongs and be created Baron Weeks.[47]

One immediate consequence for the RAOC was that the RASC vehicle depot at Feltham was added to the fold. Robby Robinson was sent down from Derby to introduce RAOC methods. Among those working with him was Stan Preston, who would take the expertise he had gained out to India in support of the 14th Army in the war against Japan.[48]

Longer term, most RAOC depots would have REME workshops within them. In spite of the division into two separate corps the men on the ground continued to work closely and harmoniously for the duration of the war.

Bill Williams strove to get the ordnance depots to work together and learn from each other. Every COO was encouraged to visit another depot each month. All the COOs met together with Bill every quarter at different depots. At this meeting there would also be Dick Hunt, previously mentioned as Bill's 'eyes and ears', John Hildreth, Bill's deputy who went on to lead the RAOC as major general, and one woman, Betty Perks, Bill's PA. General Weeks was present at some of the early meetings, notably the one held at Derby in March 1942 where the press were invited to be briefed on the activities being undertaken, particularly the supplies to Russia, which the *Picture Post* reported on 28 March 1942 with the headline 'British Generals meet to speed supplies to Russia'.

The next meeting was at Greenford in June 1942, by which time Bill had been promoted to the rank of major general and head of the RAOC. For the September meeting Longtown was chosen, and the focus was on ammunition. In July 1943, when the planning for D-Day was well under way, the COOs met at Bicester with the focus firmly on the immense task that lay ahead in getting vehicles, equipment and stores over the Channel and up the beaches under fire to equip, perhaps, a million soldiers. These meetings enabled a sharing of ideas and experience and created a strong sense of teamwork across the country.[49]

THE DESERT WAR AND ITALY

Prime Minister Winston Churchill saw the Middle East as important for many reasons. The Suez Canal would be vital to supply the Far East should the eastern reaches of the Empire come under threat. The oil reserves would be of massive benefit to the German war machine and so had to be protected. There was also the possibility, in due course, of attacking Germany from the south.

Field Marshal Wavell had taken command in the Middle East in late 1939 and in early 1940 had been joined by staff members including Dickie Richards, who headed up Ordnance Services. The British already had significant interests in the region and so there was already some military infrastructure in place. When looking at the ordnance infrastructure, it largely mirrored the Empire, since the policing undertaken by the British always required armaments. Following the end of the Great War, Britain also undertook a similar policing role for the so-called 'protectorates', such as Egypt. The infrastructure, however, was insubstantial and totally inadequate for a country on a war footing.

Richards later observed, 'It is comparatively easy to move Divisions and Army Corps from place to place, but, if they are going to be maintained, the building of roads, railways, workshops and depots must be put in hand well in advance'.[1] It was therefore remarkably fortunate that Wavell and his staff had arrived when the Italians were still posturing; they didn't declare war until June 1940.

The first decision was the location of the depots and workshops to support the tank divisions. Division commanders wanted them as close to the front as possible. Richards argued successfully that they should be kept east of the

Nile. This proved a wise decision, as they were able to support the army without interruption even when Rommel gained the upper hand.

The first task was to build the railway, since that would be the vital supply route, initially for building materials and then for ammunition and stores. Roads would follow, then buildings and finally ancillary services. The troops lived in tents for many months.[2] One of the lessons listed as learnt from the BEF was a reduced emphasis on rail; as the Desert War unfolded road, and indeed off-road, transport would improve.

THE ORDNANCE OPERATION

Under Richards' command, a Middle East ordnance organisation about the size of a large commercial business of the time was created.[3] This included four base workshops, a misnomer since not only did they repair, they also manufactured items in rubber and Bakelite, pistons and piston rings, sheet metal work, tank components, bivouac shelters and stretchers. Base ordnance depots were created at Abbassia and Tel el-Kebir, providing motor transport, clothing and general stores. Ammunition was stored over large areas above ground, but also in the Tura Caves which had been created by the quarrying of stone for the pyramids at Giza.

J.K. Stanford was posted to Tel el-Kebir and he offers a description of what awaited the party with whom he had spent the sixteen-week voyage from England:

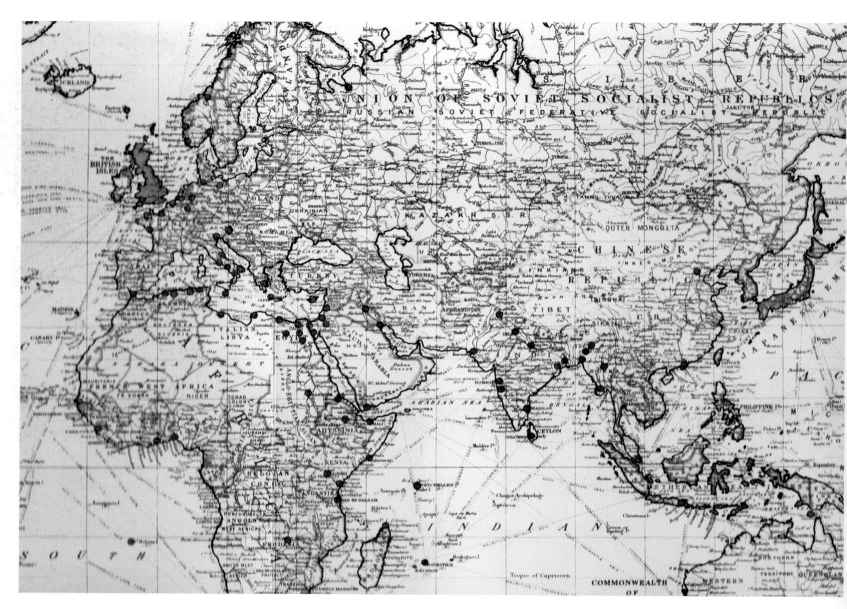

Worldwide bases, RAOC.

Tel el Kebir, seventy-five miles from Cairo, was at the western end of a chain of vast hutted camps, base hospitals, depots, workshops and prison camps. These were just springing up in the desert along the Sweetwater Canal and the Suez Road, and for years after the war became the main bone of contention between us and Egypt. They grew and grew … the desert wilderness blossomed almost as you watched.

He tells how you could see rows of buildings stretching for miles, all with water and electricity. The desert was transformed. Army lorries would bring fertile soil from the river and soldiers would spread it over the sand. Seeds would be sown and seedlings planted. Everything would be tended and soon the result was a delight: eucalyptus trees and shrubs which would grow a couple of yards a year.

Stanford's picture of daily life in Egypt before the Desert War truly got under way is one of bored leisure. General de Guingand, secretary to the Commanders-in-Chief Committee, wrote how certainly senior staff 'all lived and worked under peace conditions – except for the hours we put in … we all had something of a guilty feeling. Delightful flats with servants and plenty of food and drink.'

Some of the hours put in were filled with the energetic activity of Richards and his close team. They saw communications as vital. Again the rail links were seen as key, but supplemented by sea, given its proximity. These linked to advance bases and thence to the armies. Bases were set up in Alexandria and then planned for Tobruk, Benghazi and Tripoli – at intervals of about 300 miles. An important new element in the desert was the introduction of vehicle and stores convoy units, which added a vital element of flexibility.

For urgent demands air transport came into its own. Richards gave one particular illustration from the related Greek campaign:[4]

> The Greeks needed anti-tank rifles to hold a position against Italian light tanks. 12 anti-tank rifles were flown to an airfield in Greece from which smaller aircraft flew them to the mountain front and as a result they were in position three hours before the first tank arrived. Taken by surprise, a number of tanks were knocked out and the Italian advance held up. Greek morale rocketed as a result of this early success.

He cautioned that air transport may not be appropriate for items such as greatcoats; nevertheless, for a soldier stripping after emerging from a burning tank, replacement clothing *was* an urgent matter.

Tura Caves.

The many RAOC soldiers who served at Tel el-Kebir knew it simply as 'TK'. James Heys was posted to 2 Base Ordnance Worksop at TK on 27 April 1941. He was an apprentice painter and, not tall enough for the RAF, had joined the RAOC in September 1940. He'd spotted a notice seeking volunteers to train as mechanics, had applied and had been sent on a

Masara Caves BAD.

View of storage at Tura Caves.

ten-week course at Aldershot. After TK, where he worked on Matilda tanks, he volunteered for the Long Range Desert Group preparing motorcycles.

Some figures give a feeling for the size of the ordnance operation in the Middle East. Alan Fernyhough takes the month of El Alamein, reporting that base ordnance depots issued 29,000 tons of stores comprising 595,000 items; 68,000 tons of ammunition were issued; 1,386 new tracked vehicles and 10,600 new wheeled vehicles were received, with 809 tracked and 5,200 wheeled vehicles being returned repaired from workshops.[5]

Between May 1941 and March 1944, the Tel el-Kebir workshop completely overhauled 4,300 tracked vehicles and 19,750 wheeled vehicles, 33,500 engines and 2,300 guns. The general workshops repaired 90,000 pairs of boots and 280,000 items of clothing each month. In terms of people, in December 1940 there were 3,500 civilians and by June 1942 this had grown to 18,000 in the workshops and 20,000 in depots. In the same period the numbers of ordnance officers and men had grown from 2,000 to 47,000. Most of the civilians were local and so training was needed, both in procedures but also in English language.

It is natural for a commanding officer like Richards to paint a positive picture of his operation and there is little doubt that there is much that was very positive. Nevertheless, historian and novelist Len Deighton doesn't mince his words when he says of British supply in the early part of the desert war:[6]

Desert tank transporter. (RLC Museum)

Boot making in East Africa.

The whole British supply route from factory to desert workshops has to be blamed for any shortages of fighting equipment. In the rear areas Britain's army showed all of the bloody-mindedness and pernicious practices of pre-war trades unions.

Stanford tells how officers 'sent down to Suez for tank spares needed urgently, had to wait a day because ten tons of beer was number one priority for unloading'.

One of the gravest problems of the Desert War was the time it took to get supplies from England – some six months. As Bill Williams put it in a speech from 1942:

You can compare the problem of the pipeline to an oil well in Persia when the oil is being drawn off at Haifa. Until the pipe is filled you cannot draw off any oil. The problem of spare parts is a similar one – until we have filled the six months pipe to the Middle East we cannot draw off spare parts at the Libya end.

Somehow we have to hold the balance between over production of spares which will restrict the growth of the Army and under production which will hold up essential repair and maintenance.

Richards' response to this was to 'do it themselves', find supplies from countries closer to hand and with secure shipping routes, or to seek out local suppliers. Middle East Headquarters demanded 50,000 anti-tank mines per month and so Richards arranged for the Royal Engineers to make the mine cases and for ordnance personnel to fill them. South Africa proved an excellent source of supply using the machine tool capacity of the mining industry.[7] British East Africa was also a source of vital supplies.

When the Italians joined the war, Richards took the immediate action of acquiring some 407 vehicles in the space of a few weeks from local distributors.[8] This met an immediate need but exacerbated a larger problem with spares. The War Office had decreed that spare parts should only be provided for the current range of vehicles. In the Middle East, and indeed elsewhere in the Empire, many vehicles were too old to be on the list and so to keep them on the road much wasteful initiative was used in adapting what was available. Certainly in this opening period of the war, make-do and mend was very much the theme on which ordnance had to operate.

THE EBB AND FLOW OF BATTLE

A series of advances and retreats covering many hundreds of miles characterised the Desert War and perhaps typified what a mechanised war was like:

> The Italian Army advanced 65 miles into Egypt in September 1940. At the end of 1940 and in early 1941, the British drove the Italians westward for 340 miles, then in March–April the Italians, with decisive support of German troops under Rommel, drove the British 370 miles to the east. At the end of 1941 a British offensive forced Axis forces 340 miles back again, but in two stages, from January to February and in June 1942, Rommel reached Alamein after an eastward advance of 570 miles.[9]

We could, and indeed should, add that the Germans' first success was helped by the absence of many British and Commonwealth troops in assisting the Greeks. At sea the Germans were taken on by the navy and RAF, with varying degrees of success, in trying to ensure that supplies got through. Amid all this there was the Siege of Malta where RAOC officers and men played a distinguished role, not least in bomb disposal.[10]

In November 1940 Wavell[11] had begun his offensive against the Italians. In ten weeks his numerically inferior force defeated the much larger Italian Army. Ordnance played its part with the provision of field supply depots set up some 30 miles forward of British lines so as to be there with ammunition as the advance took place. Larger ordnance stores were provided by field maintenance centres. Shortages of MT spare parts emphasised the need for ordnance stores to be seen as different to rations, fuel and ammunition, in that they were small numbers of a great many different parts, all of which must be clearly identified and accessible when needed. The reality fell a long way short.

In early 1941 Hitler despatched Rommel and the Afrika Korps to the North African desert. From the start of German involvement, the recovery and repair of damaged tanks was an issue. Initially there were no bespoke recovery vehicles and Richards resorted to locally modified tractors. Stanford relates a story of wounded British soldiers lying at night in the battlefield waiting to be rescued but hearing all around them in the dark the Germans efficiently recovering their tanks for repair. There are repeated exchanges of correspondence in Richards' papers showing how they were trying to address the issue but with totally inadequate resources. Later in the war the muscle of Scammell recovery vehicles would be brought to bear with great effect.

The Italian invasion of Greece with the support of the Germans prompted the Greek Government to call for Allied support and, on 5 March, army units began to move across the Mediterranean to the Greek mainland. Ordnance units went with them with ninety days' worth of supplies. Both supply and maintenance had to take place within formations since the terrain did not lend itself to the traditional depot structure. It was largely German air superiority that won the day this time and ordnance units again were faced with the task of destroying the supplies they had brought. Many of those who were evacuated before the Germans could take them prisoner were taken to Crete to join the small force there.

Three weeks after their victory on the mainland the Germans invaded Crete and a similar story followed. The RAOC lost thirty-eight officers and 750 other ranks, including NCOs with valuable technical skills.[12]

Tank recovery in the desert. (RLC Museum)

Painting of tank recovery in the desert. (RLC Museum)

to develop his field force structure. This was now based on brigades, with each having their own ordnance field park (OFP), light repair section and, importantly, recovery section. There were also forward ammunition depots, communications repair sections, mobile ammunition laboratories and a vehicle and stores convoy unit. This would provide a model for the future.[15] The operation effectively ended with the lifting of the siege of Tobruk and then slowly ran out of steam.

On 7 December 1941, an event across the other side of the world was probably the turning point for the Desert War, and indeed the war as a whole. The Japanese bombing of Pearl Harbor brought the resources and muscle of the United States into the Allies' side at full force. This manifested itself in both materiel and men.

While the entry of the USA into the war was pivotal, the role played by ordinary Russian soldiers should never be forgotten and neither should other aspects of their war effort. In March 1942 Dickie Richards[16] was sent on a visit to Russia to witness the evacuation of a huge oil installation from the advancing German Army:

To technicians in our party with experience of the Oil Industry ranging from 13 to 20 years, the effect was astounding. All would have stated that it would have been impossible. Only by actual observation was it proved

In May 1993, Kostos Chrysikos wrote to the British Red Cross with his account of how, as a Boy Scout, he and fellow Scouts had aided the escape of RAOC POWs. The camp was Pavlos Melas in Stavroupolis, Thessalonika, and the Scouts aided the escape of some 100 officers and men. The Germans arrested the Scouts and Kostos, aged only 12, was spared imprisonment but given a beating that left him with spinal injuries all his life.[13]

In April and May 1941 Rommel and the Afrika Korps moved in to Cyrenaica and drove the British out of everywhere except Tobruk, which held out until November 1941 when it was relieved (making it the longest siege in in British military history).[14]

The British response came in the form of Operation Battleaxe, with Churchill replacing Wavell with Auchinleck. This was followed in November 1941 by Operation Crusader, an attack by the 8th Army. The characteristic of this operation from an ordnance point of view was the placing of field maintenance centres at intervals ahead of the British line equipped not only with rations, fuel, water and ammunition but also with those ordnance stores that were likely to be needed in the field. The four months spent planning before the start of the operation gave Richards the opportunity

Storage at Tobruk. (RLC Museum)

that it could be done. Large oil pumps had been removed, huge columns and towers had been cut in half and swung onto railway trucks; furnaces and boilers had nearly all been evacuated. Approximately 80 large tractors were working on the installation and one left with the feeling that quick decision, thorough understanding of the job and splendid discipline were combining to produce an outstandingly efficient job of work.

It may well be that this experience stiffened further Dickie's resolve to 'get things done'.

In May 1942 Rommel attacked the Gazala line. The presence of American tanks and the heavy new defence of Tobruk made the British confident of their ability to resist. In the event, Rommel succeeded tactically and was able to take Tobruk on 21 June. The 8th Army withdrew to the El Alamein line. Tobruk had become a major ordnance site and so, again, a great quantity of supplies were destroyed.

WHEELED VEHICLES

Wheeled armoured cars and scout cars proved very effective in the open expanses of the desert. Mechanised warfare was fast moving and the last thing a soldier wanted was to have to stop to change a wheel. Dunlop made

Ambulances in the desert. (RLC Museum)

a massive contribution in solving this problem with the introduction of its RF (run flat) tyre which enabled vehicles to travel up to 70 miles after their tyres had been punctured by a bullet, something that more than once saved entire squadrons of fighting vehicles from capture.

It wasn't just fighting vehicles: the British 3-ton trucks with Dunlop tyres worked tirelessly. Rommel became wise to this and issued the following order on 15 December 1941: 'For every desert reconnaissance, only captured English trucks are to be used since German trucks stick in the sand too often.' This was the result of the highly effective Dunlop sand tyre.[17]

Another challenge for motor manufacturers was sand and dust, which got everywhere and exercised its abrasive qualities to awful effect. The answer was more efficient air filters. It was a process of continuous improvement, with problems encountered in the field addressed by engineers back home. Another example stemmed from the fact that tank tracks were very effective on the desert landscape but had to be replaced after relatively short mileages. The work of British motor companies such as Scammell and Albion was vital in supplying both transporters for serviceable tanks and recovery vehicles for those damaged by enemy action.

TANKS

Following the withdrawal from Dunkirk, such Nuffield Cruiser tanks and Matildas that could be found, irrespective of condition, had been placed on-board ship and despatched for North Africa with a team of engineers charged with the task of repair and overhaul en route.[18] Further shipments followed and sufficient modern tanks had been sent to North Africa by 1 January 1941 to enable General Wavell to launch his offensive against the Italians.

Notwithstanding the successes against the Italians, shortcomings were discovered in the performance of the Nuffield tanks and a team of engineers was flown out to the desert to assess what was needed. In time, modifications were made and the relieved engineers returned home.

The story of the tank war was one of continuous experimentation and improvement. British tanks armed with 2-pounders when confronted with German tanks armed with 6-pounders were in the hopeless position of a short-armed boxer fighting a man with a much longer reach.[19] In the early days, the British tanks had to run the gauntlet of 1,000 yards in range of the enemy before they could open fire.

Nuffield subsequently dramatically revised their specification and began a production line process that would produce first the Crusader and then the Cromwell. British tanks had been outgunned by Germany's Panzers but now, with a 6lb gun, gave as good as they got. They 'had been obliged to play the role of the street urchin who pokes his head round the corner, throws a brick at the local bully and dashes off before the other can retaliate'.[20] Vauxhall's Churchill tanks joined the ranks alongside those manufactured by Nuffield and Vickers.

The American involvement brought their superior Grant and then Sherman tanks into play, which further redressed this imbalance. Nevertheless, as was clear from a report to the Armoured Fighting Vehicle Liaison Committee in 1941, the Sherman did have at least one very serious drawback, which led to its nickname, 'the Ronson': it often caught fire[21] when hit and all too often the crew failed to escape.[22]

In Prime Minister Churchill's account of the Desert War from his perspective in London, but also with his hand in their invention, tanks take on an almost iconic significance in both total numbers but also in types. When Churchill visited in early August 1941 with his prodigious command for detail, he came primed with figures of tank numbers supplied by his adviser, Professor Lindemann. The difference between these and the records held locally revealed significant shortfalls. Investigation showed these to be mainly the result of vehicles cannibalised for spare parts, but also of theft and of vehicles being categorised as BLR (beyond local repair), often a euphemism for vehicles put to unofficial uses. It was perhaps this that prompted Bill Williams to speak later of the 'waste of war'.

THE WASTE OF WAR

Waste in war is, above all, of people, and a great many lives were lost in the desert. Yet the Desert War was also typified by massive waste of materiel. In addition to the destruction of stores in retreat, this came in four guises. At its simplest there was a great deal of barefaced theft. It is undoubtedly true that local civilian employees took advantage of their position and supplemented their earnings significantly with sales of 'attractive ordnance'. It was not only locals, the impact of conscription meant that the army had within its ranks those for whom criminal activity was a norm of life. Some of these more organised men traded very large quantities and many escaped capture, so enjoying the fruits of their crimes. It would be misleading to say that the desert was uniquely bad. UK newspapers reported, week after week, prosecutions for pilfering from ordnance depots. A son of a Donnington civilian told me candidly that he thought that his late parents may well have been 'on the fiddle'. Another showed me his father's record and how he lost his stripes for 'being in possession of government property'. He later regained them and ended up as a sergeant with a glowing reference.[23] The large-scale pilfering in the Middle East was addressed, and by the time Stanford returned to Tel el-Kebir, Pathans were acting as very effective guards.

J.K. Stanford highlights a second significant area of waste, in the form of hoarding of supplies not only by individuals but by units in the field:

> There was a stealthy accumulation by all ranks of scrounged material, from blankets, vehicle cushions (as pillows), glass windscreens (to cover office tables), driving-mirrors in which to shave, or stretchers as beds, down to extra socks and shirts which could be pawned in Cairo.

One common stratagem was to mark a vehicle as being 'beyond local repair' and then either cannibalise it for parts or divert it to some non-authorised use.

Stanford tells how Dickie Richards appointed him to the post of Inspector of Army Equipment 8th Army and how he thereby discovered embarrassing quantities of all kinds of materiel. The inspection activities were so successful that returned stores sections found themselves barely able to cope with the rush. We might smile, but the truth is that hoarding on this scale necessitated the calling for supplies from the UK, which put ships and sailors at great risk. In many cases, this was simply for the additional comfort of soldiers whose lives were already a great deal more comfortable than those at home who were going without so that the soldiers in the field had all they needed.

It wasn't just the diversion of resources; it was also the risk of ships being sunk en route. Bunny Masters[24] was one a group of 200 women and children sailing round South Africa in 1942 to join husbands stationed in a number of African locations. Their ship was torpedoed and they later discovered that on board were armaments and machine tools destined for the Middle East and India. In all probability these would have originated in the Old Dalby Depot and much of the armaments in particular were only being sent because of hoarding.

The third area of waste was perhaps the biggest, and that was equipment abandoned in battle by the retreating side. There simply was not the resource to recover much of this perfectly usable equipment. Much of it remained in the desert until 1952.

A final area of wastage came from the misuse of vehicles: tanks were driven for miles on tracks rather than being transported, and once allocated to a division the maintenance of vehicles left a lot to be desired.

Waste was not only caused by lost materiel, it was also caused by equipment failing to function. It is Sod's Law that, amid massive efforts to get the right systems working, there has to be a small disaster that impacts directly on the 'boss'. The Prime Minister took a great interest in 'his' tanks and so was livid when, in December 1941, he discovered that the tanks sent from the UK had arrived rusty and needing three weeks' work to make them operable. It seems that the original plan had been for two fitters to travel with the tanks to ensure that they would be in full working order on arrival.

Churchill ordered an enquiry and Mr Justice Singleton produced a report. It seems that the whole plan had been revised over lunch at the Savoy in the middle of September. The managing director had met with a major general to see if his fitters could fly out to the Middle East instead of having to go by ship. This would enable them to be usefully employed at the factory rather than wasting time on a sea voyage. The managing director of the manufacturing company clearly needed to keep the two fitters at work in the factory for as long as possible since he added a further argument that by doing so the tanks would be completely up to date by the time they arrived in the Middle East.

Churchill, with his close relationship with the history of the tank, must have been furious. By all accounts it seems that the tanks were loaded on board ship with no one from the manufacturer present to oversee operations. To make things worse the Ordnance officer at the port did not inspect them and the staff sergeant, who did, failed to tell anyone that the tanks were not properly greased up. So if heads needed to roll, there would at least three, probably more. As it turned out, tragically, the general concerned had died in the interim and so Churchill could see no point in taking further action, having a larger war to win.[25]

This and other incidents revealed that there were clearly serious problems with the packaging and transport of stores, since officers were despatched from Chilwell to inspect and report back. Bill Williams embarked on a tour of inspection in April 1943 to find for himself what the issues were, in order to plan to address them in the forthcoming D-Day landings.

TABLES TURNING

The loss of Tobruk was followed by the replacement of Auchinleck with Alexander and the arrival of Montgomery. Richards[26] made further changes in the field support operation which contributed to Montgomery's overall success. In particular OFPs were now organised at a number of different levels: army, corps and division. With the formation of REME in October 1942, each REME workshop was given its own stores section. Vehicle and stores convoy units came into their own, adding much needed mobility that enabled supply to keep pace with the advance. Now that all vehicle supply came under the RAOC, a distinctive vehicle section began to take shape.

Other ordnance technical innovations were finding their way into the battlefield. James Childs,[27] who had joined from the Rootes Group, had become an expert in armaments and had the job of inspecting the barrels of the big guns in order to judge when replacement was required. He was issued with a motorcycle and carried his equipment (testing rods) on his back until a kind fellow officer found him a truck. The artillery was at first resistant but soon saw the benefit of being able to replace barrels before problems arose. This was perhaps another indication of the growing sophistication of the Ordnance Service.

The *John Bull* magazine[28] reported how the tables had turned:

We have beaten Rommel's men at salvaging and repairing tanks under fire this time. Our light aid detachments have carried their little forges, welding equipment and other paraphernalia into the vast swirl of desert warfare and worked under the muzzles of the German guns. They have had the joy of getting stranded tanks going again with only a minute or two to spare.

Many have been taken prisoner whilst making one last desperate effort to get the tracks roaring into movement again, and the guns spitting death.

And much more have our lads of the Royal Army Ordnance Corps accomplished in that blistering sickening heat in which man was never intended to work at all.

Delivering tanks to replace losses, they have swept straight into battle with them. They have snatched badly damaged tanks which couldn't be dealt with on the spot from under the very nose of .the enemy and whisked them away to advance workshops. And they have made sure that German tanks – possibly left in our hands very temporarily – would never move again.

I spoke to one other man back from Libya. He told me of incredible feats in the repair of British tanks – done in incredible time. 'But whereas Jerry's anti-tank guns could go through the thickest part of our armour twelve months ago, it can't today,' he said. 'And that's going to make a difference.'

Douglas Postlethwaite was one of those RAOC men who went out to tank casualties on motor bikes to troubleshoot. On one occasion he was faced with a Churchill that wouldn't start. In his training he had taken a course at Vauxhall and so was able to start it and drive the tank back to the Allied line.[29]

The success at El Alamein was followed by the first joint operation between the US and British armies in the invasion of North Africa. The invasion force, Operation Torch, carried out by some 500 ships, landed in French Morocco and Algiers and by 11 November 1942 had taken the ports of Casablanca and Bougie.

ISSUES FACED

A huge problem in supplying the army in North Africa was the shortage of shipping space. The *Times* of 17 November 1942[30] homed in on this. The background was the Battle for the Atlantic, which cost the Allies a great many ships before, with the aid of Bletchley Park, the German code was cracked and the balance of advantage won. Nevertheless, shipping space was severely limited:

Enormous strides have been made in the economy of shipping space. After the General Staff had said what shipping space was available, the problem has been to secure that none of it is wasted. This has involved the revision of the whole system of packing. A case which formerly carried one Bren gun now takes two. New systems, new methods and new types of boxes have been evolved. During the important supply period for General Montgomery's forces, tens of thousands of railway wagons packed with war stores were handled by Ordnance Depots in Britain.

The war diaries of the DOS Allied Forces HQ North Africa, Brigadier W.E.C. Picknall[31] give another sense of the issues being faced. The monthly report written to the COS War Office (Bill Williams) offers a record, but also a flavour of relationships. In March 1943 the fortnightly bulletin reported, 'Warren and McCausland have arrived and I think their visit, and that of the Chilwell party, should be most helpful'. This could be read two ways!

'Save Shipping
Space' poster.

The bulletin goes on to highlight real anxieties about MT spares and what was clearly a thorny issue of provisioning. Field depots had to be provided with the stores they needed, ideally no more and no less. Some parts would wear more quickly than others. The problem was finally addressed by creating a single provisioning activity headed by Dan Warren. The increased scale of the job was just one justification for this move. The numbers of items that had to be provisioned, and therefore whose projected use had to be estimated, had increased from 60,000 at the beginning of the war to 402,000.

Bill Williams arrived in Oran on 5 April and met Colonel Alan Fernyhough, who took him to Maison Carrée, the ordnance headquarters, where he dined with Brigadier Picknall. The following day he had a conference with McCausland and Warren at 1 BOD to receive an oral report on their visit. Later he dined with General Humphrey Gale at Allied HQ. There is no note of their conversation, but Gale would almost certainly have underlined the shortcomings of the ordnance operation.[32]

Bill went on to inspect the workshops at Constantine and those with the 6th Army. Over the next week he inspected depots, field parks, beach detachments, railhead ordnance companies, ammunition dumps and armoured workshops throughout the theatre, learning from their experience for the invasion of northern Europe. He also met the corps commanders to receive their comments on the performance of ordnance. In his brief notes on his visit, he is disarmingly frank about his perception of the abilities of his officers, ranging from 'a good type of officer and very efficient' to 'indifferent and an inefficient and untidy Ordnance unit'.

Operation Torch advanced steadily towards Tunis, which fell on 12 May with 250,000 taken prisoner. Stanford, with his inspector's hat on, was despatched to search Tripoli for valuable materiel. He reported that he found 'stacks of artillery wheels, cavalry sabres, pistol holsters, rifle stocks, anti-aircraft cannon barrels, gas cylinders and acres of mule saddlery,

Storage in Tunisia. (RLC Museum)

Mercedes Benz engines and half a million 44 gallon oil drums [the only item that could readily be used]'.

Following up behind the advance came ordnance men in support. On 11 April 1943, Geoffrey Vale,[33] an RAOC driver from Hornchurch, had boarded a requisitioned cruise liner bound for Algiers. He compiled a handwritten notebook of the period from April until September 1943. The book was not only handwritten, it had on every other page Vale's own, quite distinctive, watercolours of the places he visited. He tells how he was assigned to drive the officer commanding a vehicle park, stationed some 10 miles from Constantine, whose role it was to repair tanks. As he acknowledges, it was difficult to realise that there was a war going on; that is, apart from his record of first the invasion of Sicily and then of Italy, where British fighting divisions were the beneficiaries of the repair work. A couple of entries offer a little more flavour.

On Sunday, 23 May 1943 he set off in his Austin Utility, 'Jane', with his CO leading a convoy of two 3-ton Bedfords carrying fifty men, drivers and cooks, one water trailer and one Don R (despatch rider). They drove through 'mile after mile of golden corn, fields of vines and groves of olives … here the natives are ploughing the hillside slopes with teams of oxen and a ploughshare'.

On Saturday, 19 June:

> The Colonel OC No 1 BOD visited on his way to Bone and I drove him in his Humber 'Snipe' saloon car to HQ Vehicle park Mondovi, a Napoleonic Chateau … leaving Philippeville we took the coast road to Bougie clinging to the mountainside winding round numerous bays overlooking the sea shore … and several army rest camps with the lucky chaps enjoying themselves on the yellow sands.

SICILY AND ITALY

Away from this peaceful scene, the combined forces based in North Africa carried out two opposed landings, first in Sicily and then in Italy. A significant ordnance development was the introduction of Ordnance Beach Detachments (OBDs), whose job it was to supply both stores and ammunition across the invasion beach. Key to all this was the ability to move quickly across the beach and so stores had to be scaled back to the essentials. They had to be packed in cartons that were clearly marked and then in wooden cases with rope handles making them easy to handle.

The landings in both Sicily and Italy were successful and indeed the Italian Army capitulated relatively quickly. Hitler could not risk attack from the south and so he committed German troops to hold back the British and American advance. It would probably be true to say that the Allies thus fulfilled their objective of drawing resources away from northern Europe at which the main attack would be aimed a year or so later.

Ordnance activity in Italy was impeded from the start by a number of factors beyond their control. The headquarters remained in North Africa and the sheer distance made it very difficult to match decisions with the conditions on the ground. For example, the first depot to be set up in Italy, 557 AOD, was located at Pontecagnano, some 40 miles south of Naples, the port through which most supplies were received. Most supplies would be destined for the armies advancing to the north and so, with the need first to travel south, the line of communication was thereby extended by 80 miles. Also, the balance of activity between the east and west of Italy was out of balance with the provision of supplies.

Bedford OYD model offloading ship. (© Vauxhall Heritage Archive)

When at last ships began to arrive from Britain and the US, they had been packed without regard to the nature of the campaign being fought. This resulted in surpluses of some equipment but severe shortages of others, such as winter clothing and vehicles.

The vehicle stock of the 8th Army bore the scars of the long Desert War. Thousands of replacement engines were shipped out, but what was needed were new replacements. The fact that these weren't available was partly the result of the priority being given to the Normandy invasion but also to the lack of ordnance officers on the ground of sufficient seniority to win the arguments.

Campaigns, however, are about people. Bolton man Kenneth Lucas joined the ordnance section of Rear Army HQ as ordnance executive officer, essentially troubleshooting, but with duties including the local purchase of supplies to cover shortages in shipping from the UK. 'It was rather like running the supply office of Marks and Spencer but on a gigantic scale and, in fact, some of the staff had learned their trade in similar organisations before the war.'

One early task was the redrawing of the front, with the 8th Army moving from the central spine of Italy to the Adriatic coast. It was:

> ... an enormous logistical exercise involved in moving thousands of men, tanks, trucks and supplies over the Apennines at night so that there would be no visible movement by day ... All units and dumps had to be re-located, lines of supply altered and arranged, supplies built up for the forthcoming attack and all under conditions of maximum secrecy.

In the run-up to the attack on Rimini, he undertook the recce necessary to ensure the smooth flow of supplies.

In the winter of 1944 he was promoted to major and posted as OC Ordnance Store Section 25th Armoured Assault Brigade, 685 Tank Troops Workshop REME. The brigade was a specialist section equipped with all kinds of 'Heath Robinson' vehicles: flail tanks, bridge carriers and flamethrowers. His job was to ensure the provision of the necessary spare parts, engines and tank tracks for the REME workshop to repair damaged tanks. He recalled the giant Scammell recovery vehicles working under the cover of darkness and also the destructive powers of the equally giant tank transporters on hot country roads.

In July 1944 the new DOS, Major General Geake, who had taken over from Dickie Richards, had his headquarters moved to Caserta, south-east of

Left: Tank damage in Italy. (RLC Museum)

Below left: Tank movements in Italy. (RLC Museum)

Below: Tank recovery in Italy. (RLC Museum)

Bridging tank in Italy.
(RLC Museum)

Capua. He was now close enough to the problems on the ground to exercise the direct control that had been needed.[34]

Some of the issues faced in Italy turned out to be similar to those experienced in North Africa. Theft was a major headache, with the Italians, who had suffered from years of privation, finding the temptation of returned stores too hard to resist. On the other side of the coin, General Geake recognised as Dickie Richards had in Africa that there was little point waiting for supplies from the UK; local sourcing in Italy became a major area of activity.

General Geake was able to create a firm base in Italy from which the armies could be supplied. The Italian campaign didn't end until May 1945. It, and the experience gained in it and the previous campaigns in North Africa, provided essential lessons about ordnance that would be used to the full on D-Day.

PREPARING FOR D-DAY

I suggest that the RAOC's planning for D-Day began with the evacuation at Dunkirk. Bill Williams and his RAOC colleagues had seen the bedraggled exhausted troops come home; they were all too keenly aware of the phenomenal quantity of equipment and stores left behind and so of the need, really, to start all over again.

In the years that followed, with invasions in Africa, Sicily and Italy, much had been learnt, often painfully. So by 1943 when the 'official' planning began, Bill had already directed that 'the whole Ordnance set-up for supplying in the field should be revised'. This time the RAOC had a full role in the 21st Army Group, which was charged with the planning and execution of the invasion. Brigadier Denniston and Colonel Cutforth were the senior ordnance officers assigned.[1]

In March 1943, Bill was appointed COS in addition to his existing roles of Director of Warlike Stores and Senior Corps Officer. The buck, therefore, now stopped with him. In addition, Dickie Richards had come back from the Middle East to take up the appointment as Director of Clothing and Stores. Also, and importantly, he was to head up a Standing Committee on Ordnance Field Operations to bring to bear his experience in both the Middle East and the BEF. He was to work with Brigadier Cansdale, Deputy Controller of Ordnance Services under Bill, who had line responsibility for field operations.[2]

The new ordnance leadership faced six major tasks. First there was a packing job of monumental proportions. Then they had to be sure that they had the right amount of depot space for the invasion preparations and sufficient men and women to do a phenomenal amount of hard work. Processes for opposed beach landings would need to be worked out and ordnance men had to be trained to work effectively under fire. The supply of essential materiel, particularly vehicles and their spare parts, would need to be secured and, finally, a whole raft of final preparations addressed.

In 1941 it hadn't been just the ordnance team that were thinking ahead. Prime Minister Winston Churchill charged a young naval officer, Louis Mountbatten, with the task of thinking through the issues that a seaborne invasion of mainland Europe might present. Mountbatten came back with the single word, 'fuel'.

PLUTO

A fully mechanised army of many thousands of vehicles would need many thousands of gallons of fuel. Local supplies could not be guaranteed. Supply by tanker would only be possible when both air and sea routes were secure from enemy attack. What was needed was a piped source of fuel from which jerricans could be refilled. Land-based oil pipelines were being laid across England to bring fuel from the west coast ports. Now pipelines under the ocean (PLUTO) had to be developed.

Under great secrecy, research and experimentation began. One design involved thick rubber and lead lining, code named HAIS, the other a steel tube, code named HAMEL. The pipe had to be flexible, strong enough to resist pressure both from the pumped fuel within and from the sea outside and robust enough to survive on the sea bed driven by currents.

There were a number of other issues to address. How might such a pipe be laid? The answer was a giant 'cotton reel' dragged behind a couple of tugs. The pipe would unwind from the drum as the vessels made their way forward. The scale, though, was massive. For the shortest run, some 30 miles of pipeline would need to be wound round, and for the longer run it would be 100 miles. The fuel would need to be pumped. Therefore, powerful pumps would be needed and would have to be attached securely to the undersea pipe. At the French end, more piping would be needed to take the fuel to a place where thousands of jerricans could be filled from it. More than one pipe would be needed and probably more than one route. All work would need to be carried out under camouflage.

It was a mammoth task that employed a great many brains and skilled manufacturers. Two routes were chosen, the first from the Isle of White to Cherbourg, code named BAMBI, and the second from Dungeness to Boulogne, code named DUMBO.[3]

MULBERRY HARBOURS

Another issue identified by Louis Mountbatten and his team was the need for harbours. It simply would not be possible to land sufficient men and materiel over beaches. This became even clearer two years later on the disastrous Dieppe Raid, where fierce German resistance cost 3,000 killed or captured. In Prime Minister Churchill's words:

> [The harbours] must float up and down on the tide. The anchor problem must be mastered. The ships must have a side-flap cut in them and a drawbridge large enough to over reach the moorings of the pier. Let me have the best solutions worked out. Don't argue the matter. The difficulties will argue themselves.[4]

A Royal Engineers unit was formed with the remit to develop and then train in the use of such harbours. Churchill had foreseen problems, but the reality of the task was even greater. The beaches of northern France were subject to strong tidal flows and rough weather could not be ruled out.

A testing ground on the west side of Wigton Bay in Scotland was chosen because of its similarity and obscurity. Structures were erected, tested and driven into the rocks. Eventually a stable pier-head design was identified, called the SPUD, which drove its three feet into the sea bed to get stability. This was linked to the shore by a series of bridge spans secured on concrete 'beetles' which, on being put into position, would be flooded with sea water. The beetle closest to the shore would be of steel to avoid the erosion suffered by concrete. The problem of currents and strong seas was addressed by first sinking a line of redundant ships and then adding concrete structures known as 'phoenixes'.

The construction task was massive, involving many dry docks and other facilities around the country. It was estimated that some 40,000 men had been involved in their manufacture. Twenty-two SPUD pontoons and 10 miles of floating pier were built, as well as beetles and 210 phoenixes of sizes up to 6,000 tons.[5]

THE PACKING JOB

In an interview with the BBC at the end of May 1944[6] Hugh Searight spoke of his visit to one of the 'great depots where spare parts are packed and stored for the invasion'. The depot covered 10 square miles of countryside with its own intricate road and rail system: 46 miles of railway track and a permanent staff of 12,000 men and women. He explained:

> It is a process aided by science and the experience of the North African campaign. Stores can't be 'handled with care'; the reality is that they may well be moved under attack and are likely to stand outside in all weathers. For each item the right number per carton had to be worked out and the appropriate size and mix of cartons for packing cases decided. Clear labelling was crucial.

The *Motor Trader* magazine of 27 December 1944 brought its focus on PIP – the Preservation, Identification and Packaging of stores:

> During the early part of 1943, when the North African campaign was in progress, it was found necessary to unload stores on the beaches and to keep them in unsuitable buildings. Very soon it became apparent that the protection given to many items of equipment stored under such conditions was completely inadequate. Corrosion and breakages resulted in a tremendous loss of supplies.

This had prompted the visit in April 1943 by Bill Williams. He reported back to the Army Council, who then appointed H.G. Starley of the Champion

Sparking Plug Company to chair a committee to address the problem. The membership of the committee included Colonel Sewell, formerly of Tecalamit and then COO of COD Feltham; Colonel Robby Robinson, formerly of Dunlop and then COO of Old Dalby; and Brigadier J.W. MacKillop, a past president of the Scottish Motor Trade Association, who became officer in charge of tanks and vehicles at Chilwell.

The committee studied the problem and explored possible solutions. The studies included the chairman visiting factories in Chicago, St Louis, Rock Island, Dayton, Philadelphia, Detroit and Richmond:

It took only eight weeks for a new formula for preservation, identification and packaging to be introduced … the following steps were taken to safeguard war materials: all goods to be properly preserved before packing; goods to be packed in suitable, good quality container of the right design and strength; clear simple identification to be affixed to all goods in a way to simplify identification under all conditions.

In the wake of D-Day, a raft of articles were fed to the press. All the talk had been of the opening of the Second Front. The *Sunday Dispatch* of 2 July 1944[7]

pictured an ATS at the wheel of a Yo-yo, to us a forklift truck, but to them 'a travelling lift which picks up carries and deposits stores at the ordinance depot supplying the troops across the Channel'. The article continued:

To Sergeant Matilda Jones of the ATS, the Second Front is a very important personal matter. Her husband went to France on D-Day and she has an important job at a base ordnance depot in Southern England, the nearest to the coast of Normandy … her job is to supervise the Label Library a vast section where 80 million labels of 40,000 different varieties are filed in long rows of steel cabinets.

The *News of the World*[8] reported on the same depot, Feltham, which was leading the way in the preservation of stores:

Today I watched the girls at this depot carrying out these arrangements with meticulous care – preserving stores against corrosion and rust so that when opened they are ready for immediate use under battle conditions; stencilling and marking them so that they may instantly be identified by any soldier who may have no technical knowledge what so ever; cartoning

Schoolchildren packers.

and labelling them to ensure easy handling; packing then into special waterproof boxes so that the whole weighs not more than 100lbs.

Behind the scenes the depots had, for many months, begun the process of packing and putting together Landing Reserve (LR) sets and Beach Maintenance Packs (BMPs).

It became very clear early on that the depots simply didn't have enough pairs of hands to do this themselves. In the summer of 1943 the Derby Depot had found itself unable to deal with the volume of material it was receiving and so Colonel Robinson had the imaginative idea of seeing if schoolchildren on their summer holidays would help. The *Derby Evening Telegraph*[9] ran an article on how these schoolchildren helped to prepare for the invasion. What shone out from this was the enthusiasm and skill of all concerned, including the teachers. One girl took on the challenge of sorting a cupboard full of 30,000 boxes by size. Another group packed in three hours what their army supervisor had thought would take days. The children didn't complain of boredom since it was an activity quite different from their daily round. Peter Good, who was then at Bemrose School in Derby, remembers hot summer days packing under the supervision of ATS personnel from the Derby Depot and learning for the first time the word 'grommet'.

Gun preparation, COD Greenford.

Radio repairs, COD Greenford.

John Swan, who then lived in Leicester, remembered as a 17-year-old member of the Home Guard being bused to Old Dalby to pack crossbars for telegraph poles. John went on to volunteer for the Leicestershire Regiment and was posted to the Middle East until he was demobbed. Rugby School was also said to have been something of a trailblazer in packing work.

It wasn't just in the Midlands. The *Twickenham Times* ran this story:

Pupils of Twickenham County School for Girls and Hampton Grammar School have shown a fine sense of patriotism by giving up their Easter holiday to do war work … boys and girls aged from 14 to 16, are working morning and afternoon for the Army in packing spare parts for tanks and other Army Vehicles. … some scholars pack the spares into cartons while others seal, label and pack the cartons into boxes ready for shipment.

Elsewhere it was reported that pupils from Eton had also lent a hand at the Feltham Depot.[10]

The scale of preparations for the invasion beggars belief. Some 375 million articles including guns, tanks, wirelesses, motor vehicles and small arms were packed by volunteers in all sorts of different places: schools, fire stations, barns, Sunday schools, convalescent homes and even dance halls.[11] Soon all the RAOC depots around the country had appointed officers to gather together teams of volunteers. Their efforts made it possible for the army to have sufficient spare parts packed and ready for the invasion

THE DEPOTS

While volunteers were very important, the heaviest burden fell on the men and women working in the depots.

'No one ever hears about them; no one really cares. They do a job as gloomy, uninspiring and dull as the dust-covered crates they haul around.' A statement which begs sympathy, but hardly excites interest. Quite what the readers of the *Sunday Pictorial*[12] thought when they read it in the hot early summer of 1944 is not recorded. Though the journalist, Rex North, had plenty more to say that painted a far more vivid picture of these men and women as they played their part in the preparations for D-Day:

> At the end of every long weary day of overworked muscles, those men of the Royal Army Ordnance Corps – 'case bashers' they call themselves – are literally too tired to do anything but write a letter to the wife or go to bed. They will never go near a German for they are 'graded men', men fit only to spill sweat, not blood. Many of them could not even be put on a parade ground to march, and when we tell our children about the war we will probably forget them.

The corps was manned by a vast variety of people. These included 'graded men', those declared unfit for active service, but then also fully fit soldiers who would undergo commando training alongside their brothers in infantry and armoured battalions.

We can perhaps step into Rex's shoes as he walks round. The country is shrouded in secrecy yet everyone knows that something is happening. All along the south coast areas have been cut off so that the invasion force can be assembled. The depot that Rex visits is a hive of activity. Everyone from commanding officer down is loading onto lorries everything that will be needed: tanks and tank engines, armoured cars, tyres of all sizes. Rex meets Corporal Reg Nichols, a veteran fighting soldier, one of the many welcomed home as trainloads arrived back from Dunkirk. Now he works in an Ordnance Depot. Reg takes a break to talk about his daughter, Betty:

Now then Betty – she's five – points to the RAOC flash on her father's tunic and asks, 'What does that mean?' he says 'Regular Array of 'Orrible Cases.'

Reg looks exhausted and explains that they start work at 7.30 a.m. and are often still hard at it at 8.30 p.m. They even have their meals brought to them. Saturday, Sunday with no break. As Rex says:

> Yes, their Second Front has started. They are seeing their battles on packing cases. Not very inspiring is it? But they do it. They carry on.

A live issue in the corps, but also elsewhere in the army, was a need to identify skills and use them to everyone's advantage. Inevitably it didn't always work out in practice. Rex offers the example of Private Emptage, a gardener and a man who loved his job. Now his role is to stencil packing cases for ten hours a day. He makes no attempt to hide just how boring it is but tells Rex:

> They won't let me fight so I might as well do this job … and I have got to keep up to scratch because if I put the wrong number or letter on a packing case some unit at the front will receive a sparking plug instead of a back axle.

Dunkirk had taught the ordnance team that in operations involving short sea voyages only the essential ordnance stores should be sent to the overseas theatre and these should be supported by base ordnance depots in the UK. In July 1943 an exercise was undertaken which revealed the need for a new depot handling bulk stores. There was insufficient time to build a new depot, so some fourteen sheds were taken from CAD Bramley and these formed the new COD Basing. In a period of only two months, rail and road transport was installed, offices built and plant and machinery installed.

Basing took the strain from COD Didcot,[13] which had already set up a network of sister and sub-depots across the country. When Dickie Richards arrived home from the Middle East as DCS, he recognised an acute storage position at Didcot itself and, using only RAOC labour, built Romneys and hard standings of ½ million sq. ft. He then ordered a new depot at Thatcham providing 1 million sq. ft. Space at CAD Longtown was taken and in due course became COD Solway. Bulk stores now had a massive 16 million sq. ft of storage, one-quarter of which was under cover.

Some of the heaviest work was in the general stores depots. Rex North tells of an incident when the officer in charge thought his men needed a break and so arranged for them all to go to the cinema. In the event all but three were simply too exhausted and so went to bed.

He then came across Ted from Burton on Trent who was shifting heavy packing cases:

> … with a tool described by the Army as 'Bars, Crow, Wheeled'. The men who use them call them 'Jack Johnson' – because they will move anything.
>
> They are simply crowbars on stackers. Huge packing cases are negotiated onto them and moved around. It is a heavy tiring job.
>
> 'Do this for more than twelve hours and you have had more than enough,' Ted told me.
>
> 'Like your job?' I asked.
>
> 'Hate its guts.'

I suspect that Rex would be somewhat taken aback by this but he pressed on and discovered again that in spite of everything what mattered was winning the war, however hard the work.

By 1944 there were established ATS units at most depots and the women themselves had become fully skilled at the tasks they undertook. Rex North found a number of ATS dressed in their work uniform much like boiler suits with hair tied up. The first had been a telephonist in Rainham in Essex. She joined up to work in the offices but soon felt the need to get more hands on and so asked to work in the stores where she felt she was making a difference. Rex notes that the fact she was married to a an officer in the Sherwood Foresters was probably the driving force behind her decision. He was certain that this was the case with Doris Atkinson who was married to a Marine who had fought at Narvik, Matapan and Crete:

> Yes, these are men and women we tend to forget. But when the historical moment arrives when we set foot on the first stage of the march to Berlin, I suggest you remember this. Remember that without the sweat and toil of thousands of unsung heroes like them your son and husband would have nothing to fight with. Their private Second Front is almost over. They can do no more.

In the depots there were some 700 different makes and types of vehicle, ranging from a parachutist's folding motorcycle to a tank transporter 70ft long, including all kinds of armoured vehicle, bridge-layers, flame-throwing tanks, mobile cranes, surgeries, telephone exchanges, printing shops, pigeon vans, office lorries and bulldozers. Covered space had long since become insufficient and vehicles other than armoured fighting vehicles had been stored in the open since 1942. Somewhat later, the decision was taken also to store tanks and armoured cars outdoors. Here, hard standing was needed and so bypasses were sealed off and filled with all manner of vehicles.[14]

Herbert Ellis in *Autocar* magazine of 16 June 1944 reported on an invasion eve visit to an RAOC VRD where transport was massed for the assault on France. His article painted a picture of how vehicles were selected and prepared for battle.

The War Office had the first task of selecting the number and type of vehicle each unit was to have. This information was passed to the Central Control at Chilwell, which recorded the details and location of every one of the army's million or so vehicles. Orders for new vehicles were placed through the Ministry of Supply, but importantly the corresponding orders for the inevitable spare parts were left to the Central Control who had the data from which usage can be estimated. Vehicles were either delivered straight to units or to a VRD. These latter vehicles were essential if those damaged in battle were to be replaced quickly. VRDs stored vehicles in the open once they had been sprayed with lanolised anti-rust oil.

The VRD that Ellis visited was at the Donnington Park motor racing circuit not far from Chilwell. Vehicles were received, checked and parked. Batteries were removed and stored together in large sheds, where they were all kept on charge using diesel generators and topped up with fluid by their ATS carers. In order to minimise movement, a truck fitted with an air pump was taken round the parked vehicles to keep the tyres at the correct pressure. Radiators were drained.

The VRD also handled 'unfit' vehicles, repairing those with minor damage, scrapping those beyond repair for cannibalisation for spare parts, and sending off any in need of major repair to army auxiliary workshops. These were then brought back into the VRD for reuse. In terms of the types of vehicles, the article showed Humber Snipe staff cars, Wolseley staff cars, Austin utilities, a tourer runabout and the 'inevitable' jeep, including sea-jeeps.

PRACTICE FOR INVASION

The whole framework for supply was to be remodelled for an invasion involving a short sea voyage. The heaviest fighting would take place on a narrow strip of shore without docks and under continuous fire. Speed would be of the essence: speed in taking the stores off the landing craft, speed in getting them up the beaches and speed in stacking and sorting so that they ould be issued straight away. It wasn't just about the supply chain. It was also about packaging, where pre-cartoned boxes, waterproofed for the crossing, would double up as bins in the field depot. It was also the method by which stock could be located and controlled … under pressure.

Soldiers of the RAOC would come under just as much pressure as their fellows in infantry and armoured regiments. Accordingly, Brigadier Denniston and Colonel Cutforth decided that a priority must be 'regimental' training[15] to get them as physically fit and prepared as possible for what lay ahead. In the early part of 1944, just as assault troops were practising landings, so too were the RAOC practising the whole business of getting tons of materiel up beaches under fire. This is how *John Bull* magazine reported their training:

Nine civilians out of ten, still out of touch with the developments of modern warfare, regard the Royal Army Ordnance Corps as non-combatant!

Non-combatant! I wish they could have stood with me watching RAOC recruits undergoing Commando training. Every man has got to undergo it. For the RAOC technician of to-day has got to be a fighter as well. They go through water, barbed wire, tunnels little wider than their shoulders and then over a 12-ft. wall – all in full kit, all taking every advantage of any cover presented, and all thinking for themselves in the way demanded by the warfare of to-day. Then they have to resort to unarmed combat – real he-man stuff – to round up paratroops.

They learn how to handle every type of weapon. They study street fighting. They sleep rough in the open country. They go out campaigning for days, with nothing but iron rations for food. I repeat, this is for every Ordnance man, for every Ordnance man nowadays has got to be a fighter. And, no matter how technical his work, every man has to keep his fighting training.

That's how you breed 'em to do the magnificent work they are doing in Libya to-day.

And not only in Libya. At the huge Ordnance camp I visited I picked out one or two men who have had foreign service in this war.

One of them had played his part in the defence of a lonely African station, the name of which I mustn't mention.

The beaches of Normandy would provide the acid test of the training and preparation. The efforts of volunteer civilians, employees, soldiers and ATS personnel would, of course, come to nothing without the equipment.

SUPPLY OF ESSENTIAL MATERIEL – THE USA

The development of good working relationships with the UK motor manufacturers had produced big dividends in terms of the ease of supply. With the USA taking an increasingly important role, the time was probably overdue for efforts to create similar relationships with America's giant manufacturers. The RAOC team in the US had done good work, but now the time had come for the boss to meet his opposite numbers.

In April and May 1943 Bill Williams had visited North Africa[16] to learn at first hand the problems that faced ordnance in the three opposed landings in North Africa, Sicily and Italy. The difficulties stemmed from the invading forces needing to be able to carry out immediate repairs to equipment in the field, under fire. This meant that the right spares had to be packed, that they must be in a size of box that could readily be carried or transported up a beach under fire, that the box could be stacked so as to be accessible, that they were clearly labelled with their contents and that the contents were preserved from damage from seawater or rough handling. Spares would not be 'handled with care'.

Armed with this feedback from users he set out for a two-month trip to the United States, the purpose of which was to build relationships with the manufacturers; to see for himself US war production; to stress the importance of spare parts and to explain his new proposals for the packing and preservation of stores.

His PA prepared a full report of his visit and it is possible to read between the lines. The British were regarded as brave, but possibly second class when compared to the much better organised and equipped US Army. Bill was, by his own admission, overawed by the US: New York was quite simply unlike anything he had ever seen.[17] Nevertheless, he was not to be outdone and his tour showed a man genuinely interested in what he saw and keen to learn. Subsequent visits would see him giving very much as good as he got.

His visit followed that of Billy Rootes in November 1942, which had had the objective of cutting through the red tape holding up vital supplies. With America then in the war, its industry had to supply a growing home army as well as supporting Britain under Lend-Lease. Another issue was domestic, and this was the effective co-ordination of the British Supply Mission and British Army Staff (BAS) in the US. It seems that these two organisations were suffering from low morale, and bringing them closer together with clearer objectives resulted in a happier and more efficient programme going forward.[18]

On 17 May Bill Williams flew from Foynes, via Bathurst and Trinidad, to New York. Accompanying him was his PA, Betty Perks, and she kept a diary of the trip. They were to be the guests of General Campbell, the head of US Ordnance. On arriving in New York they were met by the press, who were keen to hear about the war at first hand and also to see for themselves a British general. In due course, Betty perfected the technique of keeping the press at bay but also on-side.

They drove into New York 'down the enormously wide streets, glittering with neon signs, crowded with people, and lined with shops full of the loveliest things, cinemas, restaurants, and what was most amazing, decorated by the most colourful taxicabs you could ever imagine'. Betty was just 24 and had never been out of Britain. They stayed at the Pennsylvania Hotel on 7th Avenue and spent a little of the next day, Saturday, 22 May, looking, or rather marvelling, at New York. Betty recorded that 'the General was as thrilled with the shops as I was'. The contrast with blitzed London must have been massive.

In Washington they met General Campbell at the Pentagon. Betty marvelled at her opposite number's office, 'beautiful walnut furniture, a lovely thick green carpet and about 20ft by 16ft in size. When I compared it with my funny little cubby-hole at the War Office, I felt a bit sick.' Bill spent the day meeting senior members of the British contingent in Washington, including General Venning, the former Quartermaster General, now with the Ministry of Supply in Washington, and General Macready, commander of BAS in North America. It appears from Betty's diary that Bill faced a certain amount of opposition from both men, but she adds, 'I think it had been a fight, but he had won over the Generals to his way of thinking'.[19] There would be further battles in the run-up to D-Day.

After three days of meetings in Washington they left for the Aberdeen Tank and Vehicle Proving Ground in Maryland, where Bill inspected West Point cadets and visited the extensive US Ordnance training establishment. He later commented, when inspecting ordnance cadets at the RAOC training school at Foremark Hall near Derby, that the British cadets compared favourably, a remark not entirely believed by Lieutenant Tom Bretherton, who attended one of the intensive Foremark courses.[20] With an establishment of 25,000 soldiers and 5,000 civilians the base far exceeded anything Britain had to offer. The Pittsburgh Post-Gazette reported on the visit with the headline, 'Briton Gets Some Yankee Pointers'.

Next was the Chester Tank Depot in Philadelphia, which modified and shipped 5,000 tanks a month. These tanks were preserved against weather and packed with all related tools and spares. The neighbouring signals depot was found to be very similar in organisation to Donnington. Next was New York and the Raritan Arsenal and the Port of Embarkation, the latter having a vehicle preparation plant to ensure that all vehicles were in working order prior to shipment.

The focus of the Canadian visit[21] was Longue Point near Montreal which was becoming the RAOC depot in Canada, receiving all Canadian production for shipment. It worked closely with BAS in Detroit. The issue, laboured long and hard, as elsewhere, was that of packing. Bill recounted tales of boxes of spares scattered on the North African quayside as field troops struggled to find the part they needed. This process had even acquired a name: 'mining'. It went without saying that this was far from satisfactory. It was no good shipping boxes of 100 of the same part. What was needed was the identification of spares into categories, based on where they would be unpacked. So, in LRs, the spares would be the most immediate, such as batteries, while BMPs would have more complex spares and only base depots would have the full set of spares needed for a complete overhaul. Where possible, spares should be packed in waterproof cartons and a scale would be provided to set out how many of each item should be in each pack. The packs would then be clearly labelled.

In Buffalo[22] he saw the production of 50-calibre guns and then at Firestone the assembly line for Bofors guns, which drew together supplies from some 600 subcontractors. The Firestone plant also majored on rubber reclamation for reuse.

The Akron Beacon Journal reported Bill's amazement at US war production at the Goodrich tyre plant. Bill stressed the need to develop artificial rubber for tyres for heavy trucks which were becoming 'more and more important'. The heavy trucks included the Diamond T 30-ton, which could carry a Sherman, and the White 920 18-ton rigid chassis transporter. There were also 'wreckers', big recovery vehicles including the Mack 5-ton 6x4, the Diamond T 4-ton 6x6 and the Ward La France 10-ton 6x6 breakdown.

The Courier Journal in Louisville quoted Bill as saying of the Hoosier Ordnance Plant and Indiana Ordnance Works:

'These plants compare favourably with anything of their kind I have seen. I was impressed not only by the facilities but by the spirit of the workers.' At the St Louis Ordnance Plant, this tall soft-spoke Britisher commented, 'there is probably no plant in the world comparable to this one. The impression it gives is of stupendous output.'

In Detroit, Bill visited Chrysler and saw a packing operation already working along the lines he had requested. He was impressed by the recycling of paint

He saw the manufacture of tank engines at the rate of sixty a day on five production lines. From Chrysler on to General Motors and amphibious trucks which performed 'amazingly' in rough seas. Again, the clear identification of spare parts was an issue. Ford were producing 500hp tank engines at a rate of twenty-five a day. Ford's River Rouge plant covered 12,000 acres and employed 100,000 men. The new Centaur tank was demonstrated, along with the production of 2in thick armour plating. The *Detroit Free Press* quoted Bill as saying, 'It's the most inspiring sight that I've ever seen'.

At the Ford Willow Run plant, Bill coined the phrase, 'Spare Parts to a vehicle are as ammunition to a gun; one without the other is useless'.[23] This was a phrase that US manufacturers would hear time and again. The issue revolved round the demands of the politicians and senior military for headline numbers of new vehicles and Bill's hard learnt lesson about just how vital spares were.

Henry Ford had been very public in his opposition to President Roosevelt's support for Great Britain. Nevertheless, with the passage of the Lend-Lease Act in March 1941, he brought to bear all the skills that had led to his peacetime success on the problem of war production, as two pieces from contemporary American magazines testify.

Time magazine in 1942 had this to say about the men who were the foundation of America's war production effort:

The Industry's front line is manned by a little battalion of unknown men in battered felt hats, sitting shirt sleeved in cubbyhole factory offices, and then darting out among the machines. These are Detroit's production men, fresh up from the ranks, a trace of grease still under their stubby fingernails. They know machines as only can men who have handled them. They are the men who plan by ear, with near-perfect pitch. With dog-eared notebooks, pencil stubs and know-how, they work out production problems that no text book could solve. These production men have the same tactile sensitivity to machinery as a surgeon has for muscle and nerve: they can make machinery and blue prints come alive as Toscanini brings notes off paper. They do not come ready made; they have to grow up with the machines.[24]

A *Life* magazine article best describes the scale of the operation at River Rouge:

The Ford Motor Company is important because it makes automobiles. To make them it has perfected a technique of mass production that long ago

revolutionised the art of industry and is now revolutionising the art of war. To make mass production more efficient, Ford built the largest integrated industrial unit the world has ever seen … There are a hundred ways in which the self-contained might of River Rouge can – and certainly will – be turned into wartime use … The first and most overpowering impact at the Rouge comes from the sheer size of the place and the things it can do – the 17 acre foundry which can produce 1,000,000 tons a day, the mechanical shovels which can grab 15 tons of ore in a single fistful, the conveyor lines which have together a length of 125 miles … Precision is at the root of all Rouge production. The plant has a special squad of inspectors who make daily tours, checking production gages against Johansson blocks. These blocks, accepted world standards of production accuracy, are correct to the millionth of an inch.[25]

The development of military vehicles including, very importantly, the Sherman tank was initially something of a joint effort between US Army Ordnance and the three major US motor manufacturers, Ford, General Motors and Chrysler.[26] Ford did, however, gain a significant advantage over the acute difficulty of sourcing engines by developing its own engine which offered the advantage of the miles that could be travelled between services and the ease of replacing parts.[27] A tank had to perform under extreme conditions and once damaged be put back into action with all possible speed.

The Ford story would be incomplete without serious mention of the jeep. Ernie Pyle, the most famous of all US Second World War correspondents, summed up the jeep:

And the jeep – good Lord, I don't think we could have won the campaign without the jeep. It did everything, went everywhere, was faithful as a dog, as strong as a mule, and agile as a goat. It consistently carried twice what it was designed for, and still kept going.

The jeep came as a result of a request from the US Army to three manufacturers, including Ford, to produce a prototype to specification for light reconnaissance and command cars. Initially Ford declined since the order was too small to make it economically viable. The order increased and Ford ended up manufacturing 44 per cent of the 647,925 jeeps built during the war.[28] An amphibious variation on the jeep was the 'seep', many of which were shipped to Russia where they were said to have been effective on the plains of the Russian Steppes.

Cutting Ford armour plate in the USA.

Jeep. (RLC Museum)

M10 tank destroyers.

The provision of spare parts was always integral to the effective supply of vehicles. In the case of the Ford armoured car, 'parts were ordered and shipped in sets of 100 requiring more than 700 types of wooden boxes with a total of 1,500 boxes filling three carloads of spare parts per set'. At a meeting later in the trip, Bill would push for greater standardisation in the packing of spare parts to meet field conditions.

Ford plants at Chester, Pennsylvania and Richmond, California, were awarded contracts by US Army Ordnance for the modification of vehicles prior to despatch. Modification could include installing flamethrowers, additional armaments and small arms as well as treating vehicles to protect them during a sea voyage, for example. General Campbell, head of US Army Ordnance, said of the Chester Depot with its 700,000 sq. ft of buildings and 62 acres, it was 'the grandest operation in all our entire military Ordnance effort'.[29]

Ford had been asked to take on the manufacture of Rolls-Royce Merlin engines, but engineers found that the Ford method of mass production was incompatible with the skilled hand-built Merlin. The answer was dictated by the shortage of skilled engineers, and resulted in the breaking down of the building process into stages of two or three tasks which could be undertaken repetitively by unskilled workers, many of them women.[30]

Ford employees might have noticed three quite particular changes brought about by war. Very many more women worked in Ford factories. At peak employment at Willow Run some 39 per cent of employees were women, working in all areas of the business. In Dagenham, by the end of the war, 10 per cent of the 34,000 strong workforce were women. Over all of the Ford plants in the US there were more than 11,000 people with disabilities, including some 1,200 partially sighted workers at Rouge alone.

General Motors took up the challenge of war by bringing to bear its network of more than 20,000 outside suppliers and subcontractors with its ninety-four plants. It also facilitated the service and maintenance of the equipment it supplied by operating training schools for US Ordnance personnel. Its production included Oerlikon and Bofors anti-aircraft and anti-tank cannons, 854,000 trucks (two-thirds of all heavy trucks produced), mobile repair shops, ambulances and field kitchens, Cadillac's M-5 light tank and Vauxhall's Churchill and the amphibian 'Duck'. All this in addition to air and sea craft.[31] During his visit, Bill inspected amphibian and truck production and M5 tank assembly. The Duck, or DUKW as it was more properly known, would play a vital role in transporting ammunition and other supplies over the Normandy beaches.

Women working at Oakland Port of Embarkation, USA.

DUKWs at work.

Chrysler had, at the request of the US Government, contracted to build the Detroit Tank Arsenal and by 1941 had produced some 729 'General Grant' 29-ton tanks which were earmarked for Britain and Russia under Lend-Lease. The Grant was succeeded by the 32-ton Sherman and then by the 43-ton Pershing. In all, Chrysler produced some 25,000 tanks.

It produced 60,000 Bofors guns, often mounted on a four-wheel chassis or in pairs as anti-aircraft 'pom-pom' guns. Add to this searchlights and mobile radar, 438,000 army trucks and millions of rounds of ammunition. An unsung hero was the marine tractor, with one or two engines, often referred to as the Sea-Mule.

Bill visited the tank arsenal and noted afterwards:

This plant symbolises the highest perfection of American organising ability ... speed with safety and efficiency and the ever constant desire for improvement for one single purpose – to produce the greatest possible number of tanks as a contribution not only to the war effort but to early victory.[32]

Crusader and Sherman tanks, USA.

Richmond Tank Depot, USA.

The plant was clearly vast and completely mechanised with an overhead monorail and machines that cut through armour plating at the same speed as production machines cut through sheet steel. The plant used a flow system of production, with banks and banks of the same machine doing the same work, all arranged together as one producing unit. Bill inspected the eighty test tracks and both he and his PA put on gleaming white overalls to test-drive Shermans.

The *San Francisco News*[33] reported of Bill, 'He left North Africa six weeks ago, having gone there to get what he calls "the customer viewpoint" about how the equipment is proving out under actual campaign conditions'. They quoted him as saying of the Allied victory in North Africa, 'a magnificent example of United States, British and French co-operation and a tribute to American equipment'. He singled out the Sherman tank and the jeep, 'especially when driven by a WAAC, but who doesn't!' The *Los Angeles Examiner* put it even more strongly, 'American made weapons played the major role in the Allied victory in North Africa. General Sherman tanks are the best in the world. They completely smashed Rommel's Panzer divisions.'

Bill Williams at Chrysler, USA.

Other places included in the trip were a Hoover plant given over to war production, the manufacture of fabric and the organisation of the US quartermaster depot of general stores. There was also time for a little relaxation.

A key meeting on the trip took place coincidentally on Bill's 52nd birthday, when the Americans highlighted that the core problem with spares was the sheer number of different items.[34] The meeting agreed a rationalisation into the categories of urgency that Bill had proposed. The record of two major speeches given by Bill, the first to senior Canadian Ordnance officers and the second to US Ordnance officers in Detroit, highlight some of the challenges.[35] To the Canadians he was at pains to stress that there was one war and so it made sense for ordnance organisations to work together and, where appropriate, amalgamate. He told his audience that while visiting the depots and plants he had picked up many helpful ideas of good practice: 'They are perhaps only little things but they all lead to the efficiency of the show. I am a great believer in this system of interchange of ideas.'

To the Americans, it was again spare parts: 'It is only when you see vehicles, tanks, guns and other equipment on the lines of communication out of action for want of spare parts that you realise the importance of adequate spare parts supply.' He equated this to the supply of ammunition:

> You may only use a small percentage of the quantities produced, but you must have spares like ammunition spread in adequate quantities all over the supply lines and at the bases. The right part, in the right place at the right time.

Less than eight months after he returned to the UK, Bill again flew over to the US to 'loosen up some bottlenecks in industry', this time armed with a letter from General Montgomery at Headquarters, 21 Army Group, and dated 14 March 1944.[36]

In the letter General Montgomery explains his serious concern that there are shortages of spare parts and equipment for tanks and vehicles. He, in effect, repeats Bill's own mantra that spare parts are essential and without them the planned operations could be seriously affected. The letter was clearly intended to be shown to anyone challenging Bill's requests, since Montgomery says with total clarity that Major General Williams is representing his interests.

The trip this time lasted from 28 March until 7 April. First on the list was the office of the chief of ordnance in Detroit.[37] The most severe shortages were of engines for Sherman tanks and spares for DUKWs. While Chrysler

Generals Williams and Simpson with Ingrid Bergman.

had visited the UK to see the problem for themselves, it seems that the position with Ford spares was challenging. Spare batteries were critical, as were very large recovery vehicles. The problem was with production and the competing demands of the British and US armies. It is interesting to note that Bill's opposite number, General Campbell, had given his permission for Bill to visit the manufacturers again.

The first was Ford, attended by Henry Ford II among others, where Bill illustrated the problem by saying that the landing reserves and beach maintenance packs for the invasion were currently incomplete because of the absence of essential spare parts.[38] Particular problems were occurring with bearings because of the poor quality of metal available but also, it transpired, procurement procedures.

The second meeting with General Motors focussed on the problem of DUKW spares, tank engines and batteries. Chrysler, again, seemed to present the least difficulty. The issue with Continental Motors in Detroit was rates of wear, particularly of gaskets. The problems with Canada revolved round the new packing procedures.

Visits to Firestone and Goodrich brought updates on synthetic rubber production.[39] The visit to the Chester Tank Depot addressed a problem of missing parts that boiled down to a misunderstanding with the parts list. The final visit, to the Electric Storage Battery Company, found a solution to the shortage of spare batteries.

None of this seems earth-shattering but, as Bill said, a vehicle without spares is a gun without ammunition – useless.

He was again accompanied by Miss Perks, but this time also by Brigadier Alex Abel Smith, now head of British Ordnance in the US and perhaps able to open doors with the combination of his education at Eton and Magdalen Oxford and his marriage into a North Carolina family. One of Bill's later favoured sayings was, 'It is not what you know that matters; it is who you know'.

Dickie Richards, as Director of Clothing and Stores, visited the USA and Canada from 27 January to 3 March 1944 accompanied by Major G.K. Findlay. He visited the Quartermaster Stores depots, the ports of embarkation, the Aberdeen Proving Ground and laboratories in and around Boston, including a visit to Harvard to look at climatic research. Mechanisation, in the sense of the application of technology, was reaching all points of the ordnance operation.

Visit to Austin Motors, June 1944.

SUPPLY OF ESSENTIAL MATERIEL – UK MOTOR MANUFACTURERS

In parallel with this activity in the USA, UK manufacturers were sparing no effort in meeting the demand for supplies that the plan for D-Day placed upon them. A key task for motor manufacturers was the development of waterproofing for vehicles. There would be no port, and so vehicles would roll straight off landing craft into seawater before making their way up the beaches.

The War Office called manufacturers to a conference and in 1942 commissioned the development of new ways of waterproofing vehicles. The immediate task was to keep water away from the ignition and electrical components while the vehicle was submerged. The carburettor had to be protected and air inlets were needed both for the engine and cooling system (in tanks). Experiments proved that there was no such problem with exhausts, which would 'gurgle away' under water. Seawater also rusts and breaks up lubrication and so protection was needed for axles and gearboxes. Tank turrets and guns had to be sealed and the seals had to be removable from the inside, since tanks running up a beach would be in action straight away.

Morris undertook the development of waterproofing techniques that would make machines watertight up to a height of 6ft. The techniques were then passed, under tight security, to subcontractors who would undertake part of the process.[40] Care was taken to ensure that no one saw the whole picture. Morris also produced Salamander and Neptune amphibious vehicles.

Ford at Dagenham developed means by which vehicles could be waterproofed with a compound known as Trinadite to avoid the problems experienced in Sicily and North Africa.

Vauxhall had been asked to replicate the German all-purpose 88mm gun. A number of captured guns were delivered to Luton and stripped down. Prototypes were produced using existing Bedford engines. The company was just about ready to go into production on VE Day.

In relation to the RAOC itself, West Hallam undertook the waterproofing of armoured vehicles and Feltham, with more than a guiding hand from Chilwell, handled wheeled vehicles. As early as October 1943 the *Nottingham*

Evening News had reported on ATS girls working on 'secret kits' at the West Hallam sub-depot.[41] The purpose of this secret activity was to enable tanks, lorries and armoured fighting vehicles to launch from landing craft on to the beaches.

While the Americans were spearheading the development of artificial rubber, Dunlop made great strides in what we would now call recycling, grinding down old tyres and using the material to make new. It also made a major contribution through the manufacture of decoys 'which when inflated almost exactly duplicated a Sherman tank and could be packed in a hold–all a little larger than a cricket bag. Its weight was 170lbs, compared to the 35 tons of a Sherman.'

SUPPLY OF ESSENTIAL MATERIEL – THE SPECIAL VEHICLES

Preparation for D-Day exercised some of the best brains in the country, not least on adapting vehicles to unusual uses, and reference has already been made to some of the adaptions made to Churchill tanks. The challenge facing vehicles was the same as that facing the invasion as a whole. The advance would begin in water and then would need to progress over sand, which may well have been mined, then on through heavy defences. Max Hastings, in *Overlord*, described what happened on Sword Beach. He told how the special vehicles came from the landing crafts whirling chains thrashing the sand to explode any mines that might have been laid. These Shermans then resumed their main function as tanks and fired at the German defences. It was horrific, as Hastings explains:

> Mundy could hear screams from defensive positions above the beach as a Crocodile flame-thrower puffed its terrible jet of fire towards them. 34 of the 40 Sherman DD amphibious tanks launched against Sword also arrived as planned, ahead of infantry, cleared the beach successfully and became heavily engaged in the dunes beyond.[42]

Not every part of the invasion happened according to plan like this, however it illustrates the process of putting armour first to make safe the territory for the infantry. The Crocodile was a Sherman tank pulling a tracked trailer of flammable fluid. As well as tanks fronted with flails, there were those with bulldozer attachments for clearing roads, those with bridging material for crossing streams and ditches, and those that could lay tracks over sand to provide a sure footing for what followed. The 'DD' stood for Duplex Drive; these Sherman tanks were fitted with propellers and a waterproof skirt, enabling them to come off landing craft into the sea and 'swim' to the shore ready to engage the enemy.

Another ingenious vehicle came about because of the arrival of a better alternative. The better alternative was the British 25-pounder towed gun which replaced the Canadian-made Priest tank. Mechanics at a field workshop removed the existing gun from the Priest chassis, which was then used as a troop carrier called a Kangaroo. There was also the Canal Defence searchlight mounted on a Grant tank, the Buffalo amphibious landing tracked vehicle, and a good many more.

These vehicles were all part of the 79th Armoured Division, under the command of Sir Percy Hobart, which had been formed specifically with D-Day in mind. It didn't operate as a single division, rather it was distributed across the various divisions taking part in the invasion. The vehicles were known as 'Hobart's funnies'. The Sherman Firefly was probably not a 'funny', but was an adaption of the US Sherman, having its 75mm gun replaced with the superior 3in, 17-pounder anti-tank gun, and was a firm favourite of British tank crews. All these vehicles were handled through COD Donnington.

In terms of other unusual equipment, Airborne divisions would have folding and standard bicycles and light motorcycles, and Tetrarch light tanks (replaced by Cromwell cruisers in July 1944).[43]

This was just the work going into motor vehicles. Royal Ordnance factories were working round the clock to produce ammunition. CAD Corsham was working at full tilt supplying ammunition to the 21st Army Group, but also to the forces in Italy and those preparing for war in the Far East. Corsham also supplied the RAF with the bombs they would need to support the invasion force. Elsewhere, clothing manufacturers were producing uniforms by the ton, and everything needed to be packed and transported.

FINAL PREPARATIONS

Depot structures had been worked out: COD Greenford was to be the focus for armaments and technical stores and the first port of call for demands from the advance depots over the Channel. COD Feltham, as the southern part of the Chilwell network, was to be the focus for vehicles. COD Bicester provided back-up for both. Indeed, all depots around the country had their focus on supplying the 21st Army Group.

The National Archives have preserved the war diaries of the CODs for the early part of 1944. Reddy Readman at Chilwell wrote his as a management report with a focus on numbers; we might view them as 'key performance indicators'. In April 1944 he reported that, during the month, some 17,573,206 items had been packed in cartons bringing the total to date to 143,643,187 using some 6,265,340 cartons. He reported on the printing of labels, which was saving many man-hours. The printing department at Chilwell had expanded into an operation employing some 250 people.[44]

Earlier he had cautioned on the slow arrival of spares from the US, but now reported that, as a result of the visit by the COS, spares were arriving in greater numbers. Nevertheless, in June the spares position with the White personnel carrier, Mack breakdown vehicles and Diamond T transporters was still urgent; if this remained the position, some vehicles would need to be cannibalised for spares. It is also clear from his report that the field operations were being put together ready for transit on and after D-Day. The AODs were staffed and supplies were being earmarked. The same was the case for the forward trailer sections and ordnance field parks as well as for the landing reserves and beach maintenance packs. Of crucial importance, he reported that work on wading and ventilation equipment was complete and so the department could stand down.

The diaries for both COD Donnington and COD Bicester were written by regular soldiers. They were in the style of factual accounts of activity. Donnington's focussed on the equipment it was handling, including many of Hobart's 'funnies'. Bicester was exercised by staff shortages, a theme echoed throughout the depots in the first part of 1944. It was also dealing with the rush of equipment from the USA.

Derby was commanded by Robby Robinson, who had come to the army from Dunlop. The tone, and indeed content, of his reports were wholly different. The first matters covered were entertainment and sport, followed by depot staff. For example, in January 1944 there was a 'book week' and *Music While you Work* was broadcast over the tannoy with some words of introduction by the CO. There were then reports on education opportunities before getting to the detail of the business of the depot. Even here, there was a touch of civilian management. Photographs of the vehicle, scout car or tank for which spares were destined were exhibited at the end of the respective rows of bins where the packing was taking place and this 'greatly stimulate interest in the job'.

The February report covered the Derby Debating Society on the motion 'Conscription should be continued after the war'. In relation to business, the packing of landing reserves and beach maintenance packs was reported. March saw a great increase in the overtime required and a system of redeployment of clerical staff to store duties when needed. As well as *Music While you Work* haircuts were offered during working hours, given the demands of overtime. As elsewhere, there were poster campaigns, but at Derby these included ones for war charities and blood donation.

All around the depots the pace of activity was growing. Maisie Waggott who had joined Chilwell in 1938, spoke of the increase in work hours in early 1944 with twenty-four-hour working in two months of days followed by one month of nights. The sheds were cold, but lightened, as in Derby, by *Music While you Work*. The morale-boosting presence of her immediate boss, Colonel McCausland, clearly had a big influence.[45] Maisie remembered the drone of planes flying overhead on the night of 5 June.

Vehicles and stores were now being put in place alongside the waiting troops in the embarkation areas along the south coast, marked on the map like sausages.[46] In Cornwall, from where many Americans would depart, Tiny Rundle, then a land girl, remembered the rumble of vehicle engines on the road. Everyone knew that something very big was about to happen.

7

D-DAY AND THE BATTLE FOR EUROPE

I try to imagine Brigadier Denniston and Colonel Cutforth in the early hours of 6 June, unable to sleep but equally unable to do anything more. Months of preparation and planning now had to stand or fall, measured only by results.

I can more easily picture Colonel Cutforth since, as a child, I met him some years later when he had risen to the rank of major general and had been knighted. Sir Lancelot Cutforth, to a small boy, was all 'King Arthur and the Round Table' and, from memory, Sir Lancelot did not disappoint. He was a tall, dignified figure who, as a younger man, must have been the quintessential dashing army officer. His role though, with Brigadier Denniston, had been one of painstaking planning.

The 21st Army Group, which they supported, comprised the British 2nd Army and the Canadian 1st Army, each with their ordnance units. Brigadiers C.H. Clark and J.A.W. Bennett were the respective deputy directors of Ordnance Services. Brigadier Clark had been on the disastrous Norway campaign with Colonel Cutforth and then had played a key role in North Africa.

I try also to imagine Bill Williams and Dickie Richards. Bill, in particular, who would carry the can if things did not go well. They too had done all they could. In the planning, the question of morale had ranked high and so Dickie's Depots', supplying camp and laundry equipment and especially clothing, were in no sense less important than those supplying warlike stores. In any event, all stores had to cross the Channel and make it up the beaches.

Perhaps the question to the fore of each of their minds was whether, this time, mechanisation would truly work.

D-Day is the story of many thousands of men and women: Stan Carter[1] was a private with 11 Ordnance Beach Detachment, Arthur Beards was a despatch rider with 14 AOD and John Frost was a private with the ordnance field park attached to 11th Armoured Division. Their roles illustrate the stages of supply and their stories put a little paint between the lines.

First, though, an account of what mechanisation actually felt like from a young driver of an armoured vehicle.[2] Matthew Guymer was posted to D Squadron of 11th Hussars the day after his 20th birthday and a matter of weeks before D-Day. He later transferred to the RAOC. He recalled his first few weeks with the Hussars getting to know the vehicles: Daimler armoured cars and scout cars, Staghound armoured cars, Humber scout cars and American White Company scout cars. He also carried out the waterproofing for wading ashore. This was brought into sharp focus as he prepared to drive off the landing craft on to which his Humber scout car had been craned from the ship on which they had crossed the Channel:

I looked toward the beach and saw to my horror and surprise that we were much further from the shore than we had been told to expect (800 yards rather than 200–300). With heart racing and adrenaline pumping at full blast I drove down the ramp into the water, hoping and silently praying that I had carried out the waterproofing of my car successfully. The skipper waited as we drove slowly down the ramp into the water to see if he had picked a good position to offload us into the sea before releasing the other vehicles on board. He must have realised that he had put us down on a sandbar because he saw us drive off into very deep water and I was soon within the last inch or two of my sea wading capability. The rough sea was almost up to the top of the specially erected wood and canvas structure, built on top of the officer's sliding roof hatch of our HSCs (rather like a submarine conning tower). These gave us the ability to wade through deeper water. Our height was now less than two metres, but even so driving in that rough sea was a bit hairy because some water did come into the car over the top of the 'conning tower'. Because the car was completely submerged, all I could see was the water lapping against my glass visor as I kept the car moving steadily over the seabed toward the shore.

What followed was much, much worse. The part of the beach where they had landed turned out to be soft sand and the car sank with wheels spinning. They had to wait until evening before the Beach Master came along and pulled them out. Thereafter, as front vehicle in their squadron, they were in constant danger of taking the first shot from German guns. They witnessed the most dreadful destruction and carnage as they fought their way slowly to Hamburg, where their general finally negotiated the surrender on 3 May 1945.[3]

Humber armoured car.

THE ORDNANCE BEACH DETACHMENTS

The job of OBDs was to follow on quickly behind the assault troops and set up ammunition dumps just behind the beaches ready to issue ammunition to replace that used in the initial assault. Stan Carter had boarded a landing craft at Tilbury loaded with 200 tons of ammunition destined for the Airborne Division, which had flown in by glider to take Pegasus Bridge.

Sword Beach. (RLC Museum)

Open storage, Normandy, 30 June 1944. (RLC Museum)

The 21st Army Group[4] was to invade three beaches: Gold, Juno and Sword. Each beach had attached to it OBDs and ammunition companies. Advance parties came ashore within an hour or so of the first assault troops and created sector dumps just off the beaches. The main stocks were anti-tank and anti-aircraft ammunition; landing reserves followed, and stretchers and blankets for casualties and survivor kits. These latter were complete changes of clothing and kit for soldiers who had experienced a 'bad' landing. Landing reserves were designed to supply troops with spare parts for the first four weeks and comprised 8,000 cases calculated to maintain a brigade.

Stan[5] had been promised a dry landing, but in the event was offloaded into 5ft of water some 15 yards from the sand. To make matters worse his job, with one other, was to pull a handcart carrying the ammunition from the craft up the beach to the dump, and all under mortar fire.

Accounts of other landing craft laden with ammunition talk of DUKWs being used to transport them across the beach. I noted, from the war diaries of Brigadier Readman at Chilwell[6], that right up to D-Day there had been a problem with supplies of DUKWs. Perhaps Stan's craft drew the short straw and so ended up with the handcart.

Just as Stan made it up the beach the first time, the Bren carrier next to him ran over a mine and some of the resulting shrapnel embedded itself in Stan's thigh. He didn't remember pain, rather the need, with his mates, to get on with the job. The ammunition was duly stacked and issues made, again all done under fire from German mortars only yards in front. Stan recalled that once on the beach all the good intentions to keep records of issues went out of the window.

A mortar hit an adjacent petrol dump and burning petrol spread towards the ammunition. Stan spoke of his captain's bravery in putting out the fire with his bare hands, an act which cost Captain Thompson his life. The wound in Stan's thigh couldn't be left and so he was taken to the field dressing station and from there back to England. He did return to France and his story continues later.

On D-Day, 59,000 personnel, 8,900 vehicles and 1,900 tons of stores had landed; by day fifty after D-Day (D +50) this had increased to 631,000 personnel, 153,000 vehicles and 689,000 tons of stores.[7]

Bill Williams speaking at Halifax.

THE COST OF WAR

None of this materiel was without cost. Early in the war, Bill Williams had spoken at a number of depots to thank them for raising money to buy tanks. In June 1944, following a visit to Arromanches to inspect progress, he went to Halifax and a number of other towns to encourage citizens to put money into war savings.

THE MULBERRY HARBOURS

Bill visited Arromanches within seven days of D-Day and witnessed the construction of its Mulberry harbour. In his book, *Road to Berlin*, George Forty says this of the two Mulberry harbours:

Mulberry harbour panorama. (RLC Museum)

Mulberry harbour unloading. (RLC Museum)

Each harbour was as large as Gibraltar Harbour, with iron breakwaters weighing 3,000 tons and vast concrete caissons, some of them 400ft in length. They were designed to land 12,000 tons of stores and 2,500 vehicles daily.

A storm that began on 19 June and blew for three days wrecked the harbour on Omaha, but the one at Arromanches was salvaged and continued to operate.

HAMEL PIPELINE

On a later visit in July, Bill would also have seen pipes carrying fuel over the Normandy beaches, but attached to a tanker anchored offshore, rather than to the PLUTO pipeline as planned; a risky but essential venture.

The main problem in laying the pipeline had been the length of time it took to secure Cherbourg. Nevertheless, from 18 September, with a port secured and problems overcome, fuel did begin to flow at a rate of 56,000 gallons a day through a HAIS pipeline. The fuel was piped up to fields behind the beaches where men of the Pioneer Corps filled thousands of jerricans. On 29 September, a length of the HAMEL pipeline was laid and fuel soon began to flow through it. A decision was made to increase the pressure and in quick succession both pipelines failed. With the war now some miles to the east, no attempt at repair was made. For the time being, all fuel would arrive by ship.

THE ADVANCE ORDNANCE DEPOTS

The Advance Ordnance Depot (AOD) was the unit that would follow the OBDs once the landing had been secured. Brigadier Denniston and Colonel Cutforth had decided that the 21st Army Group[8] would be best served by having four such units (numbered 14, 15, 16 and 17). The plan was for 16 and 17 to set up together behind the beaches, 14 would set up in Caen and 15 would be kept in reserve.

The recce party of 17 AOD, consisting of sixteen officers and nine other ranks, had embarked on 7 June. The craft they were sailing in was hit, with the loss of all officers except for the COO. A reserve recce party was phased in but didn't arrive until the same day as the advance party on D +7 (day 7 after D-Day). The site for the depot was identified at Vaux-sur-Aure and

14 AOD. (Arthur Beards)

prepared, and the full party supplemented with staff from 16 AOD arrived as planned on D +10. Royal Engineers worked on improving road access and in spite of dreadful weather 19,000 tons of stores had been received by the end of June. The depot took over issues from the OBDs at the beginning of July and continued until 14 September.

The plan was that for the first thirty days the AOD would be supplied from BMPs, each weighing 500 tons and comprising 12,000 cases. With both LRs and BMPs, cases were limited in size and weight and could be stacked for use as bins. There then followed Standard Maintenance Packs (SMPs) containing spare parts for heavy artillery, signal and wireless stores, clothing and general stores. Finally, OFPs landed, complete with spare parts and equipment such as guns and small arms, wireless sets and vehicles for issue to units. A slight variation on OFPs were Forward Trailer Sections (FTSs), which would follow advancing tank divisions on breakout.

Caen was to be taken on D-Day itself. In the event, the German Panzer division offered stiff resistance which kept the Allies back until mid-July. Nevertheless, the landing of troops continued and with this their need to be supplied. Pressure built on Brigadier Denniston to decide whether to wait until Caen was taken before setting up 14 AOD or to select a different site to relieve the pressure more quickly. He decided on the latter and a low-lying site was selected some 5,000 yards from the German position. The weather once again was the more effective enemy and the site soon became a sea of mud. Colonel Bob Hiam had been chosen to command 14 AOD, bringing his extensive experience of operating COD Old Dalby. Royal Engineers performed minor miracles in getting the site operable and the necessary staffing was provided by drawing on 15 AOD, recruiting French civilians and drafting in German POWs. The depot took over issues on 14 September.

Arthur Beards,[9] the son of a West Bromwich policeman, had been posted to 14 AOD near Donnington when it was formed in the spring of 1943. He had been called up that winter and had spent a cold, wet few weeks of training near Blackpool with daily morning runs to Lytham St Anne's and 10-mile marches to the rifle range. At that time, 14 AOD was about 100-strong under Major Baker, a former Woolworths manager.

Arthur had been a lorry driver and so was chosen to go on the army drivers' course at Sheffield. From here he volunteered to train as a despatch rider and remembered being dropped off a lorry with his bike, a map and a map reference and being told to find his way back to base – not a problem.

Arthur Beards.
(Arthur Beards)

He became Major Baker's driver when the AOD moved to Derby and he recalled taking him to a big conference at Chilwell (we might suppose part of the D-Day planning).

He also remembered visiting Woolwich Arsenal, then bulging with stores and armaments for the invasion. 14 AOD embarked at Tilbury, and Arthur later told his grandson of his crossing and landing:

Each of the bigger landing craft had a tiny galley. On the way over there I got talking with one of the crew and told him I was hungry. Lots of the lads were throwing up but I was just really hungry. He said 'What size pumps are you?' So I told him I was a ten. He said 'Lovely, so am I. How about you give me your pumps and I'll knock you up sausage and chips? Slip into the galley in 15-minutes.'

So I did and he'd done me sausage and chips. We were all heading to the beaches to face who knew what, and I was eating sausage and chips.

When I'd finished, I went into my kit bag and handed him my pumps. He said, 'You could get put on a charge for this, you know?' and I said, 'Well it's a bit late now, what are they going to do, send me back? We'll be there in an hour.'

And he said, 'True. And let's face it, you'll probably not be around long enough to use them, anyway' (he breaks off from the story at this point and laughs, really laughs, then, as the laughter subsides, his face drops). 'An hour later, I was trying to get a tractor up the beach and it got stuck in the sand. I looked up and saw planes overhead turn into fireballs.'

Arthur's war came to an end when he was on his way to Amiens with messages for the OFP, as he had done many times. He had no idea what happened, but he woke in a field hospital and remembered two identical nurses standing at the foot of his bed – a double vision that is still with him seventy years later. It took two years for his leg to heal and he can show you the plate and screws and also the bone graft taken from the other leg.

This sacrifice by a young man demonstrates one of the 'wastes of war'; Bill Williams referred to others in his speech for Salute the Soldier Week in Halifax:[10]

Now, war in itself is essentially wasteful and if we are to be victorious we must not waste, or what appears to be waste, more than the enemy. This is the cost of war.

It is rather like a business: you have two courses open to you, either you carry on with your old-fashioned plant and gradually fall behind in the race, or you constantly install the very latest and best plant, and thus get ahead of your rivals. So it is in war. It is even more essential; in fact it is vital that we should be ahead of the enemy in all of our equipment.

The effectiveness of people's savings and the resulting supply of equipment was affirmed by Max Hastings in his book *Overlord*. He describes the sight of dumps of fuel, stacks of ammunition, tanks straight from the factory parked in neat rows and crowded in fields:

To almost every man of the Allied Armies, the predominant memory of the campaign, beyond the horror of battle, was the astounding efficiency of the supply services … for young British soldiers, who had grown up with the legend of the War Office's chronic bungling, and of the Crimea and the Boer War, Second Army's administration in Normandy seemed a miracle.[11]

He quotes Alf Lee of the Middlesex Regiment as saying:

> Whenever you went to the rear and saw fields packed with petrol cans as high as a house, rows of guns under canvas covered waiting to come up, huge dumps of shells, you couldn't doubt that we could do it.[12]

VEHICLE COMPANIES

14 AOD continued as the principal source of supply until the Allies secured Antwerp as the new base for the advance depot. The original plan was for each AOD to have a vehicle company attached to it. The companies were split into vehicle parks and comprised the full range of reserve vehicles needed to replace vehicles lost in battle.

The shipping of 17 Vehicle Company was to begin on D +2 and continue until D +17. The vehicle company recce party was lost with that of the AOD, nevertheless the first reserve vehicle issues were made on D +6. Vehicle

Pioneers filling jerricans. (RLC Museum)

DUKW park, northern France. (RLC Museum)

companies still in the UK continued with the waterproofing of their vehicles. The creation, on D +25, of a pier (the Mulberry harbour) to take vehicles directly from ships made waterproofing less necessary and was hailed with a huge sigh of relief from drivers.

Notwithstanding the presence of four vehicle companies, the major challenge for the RAOC within the campaign would be a shortage of transport. Accordingly, no vehicles were brought over empty and none remained loaded longer than was necessary. The vehicle companies were supported by VRDs in the UK. With the breakout on the taking of Caen, the need for mobility became paramount and so the vehicle companies were brought together under a single command and were thus better able to support the advancing troops.

ORDNANCE FIELD PARKS AND THE ADVANCE

John Frost[13] had been posted from Old Dalby as storeman to the OFP attached to the 11th Armoured Division. The field park was a mobile storeroom – a group of lorries fitted out with bins carrying the spare parts most commonly needed by the armoured division. It had come together in 1942 and had been stocked and trained to be ready for deployment when the time came. It too sailed from Tilbury. John remembered the journey round the North Circular, with crowds of people waving flags and offering cups of tea as the convoy made its slow passage. It also passed the Ford factory in Dagenham where the workers had rigged up a banner bearing the words 'Good Luck Boys'.

John's landing craft did manage a dry landing and he and his convoy were able to drive up the beach and a mile inland before stopping to form up. His unit followed the armour wherever it went. He would sleep on a stretcher in the back of his lorry, surrounded by his treasured stock records. He recalled the advance through France and how, particularly through mile after mile of devastated farmland, it didn't feel like being in an army of liberation at all. This changed on crossing the Belgian border at the end of August where they were met by cheering crowds.

Another feature of the advance was the impact of RAOC mobile laundry and bath units. 'The faces of battle-worn veterans broke into smiles when they caught a glimpse of the showers and realised they were not dreaming – there really was a chance of a bath here and a change of clothing.' There is a story of a bath unit which managed to get ahead of the advancing troops

it was there to serve. It managed to set up with hot water ready for the troops when they arrived. Mobile laundries were also a vital part of hospital provision. Smaller mobile units were provided for hospitals for the first two months after D-Day, with a much larger permanent base laundry following. The fall of Caen gave the opportunity for civilian laundries to be taken into use and released mobile units to go ahead with the advance.

The 11th Armoured Division entered Antwerp on 4 September and was followed swiftly by the reconnaissance party of 15 AOD, which had been held in reserve since D-Day. The COO, Colonel Volkers, and his senior team began to identify and secure the vast amount of accommodation they would need. This was done while Antwerp was still under fire from German positions on the opposite side of the Scheldt, with the Canadian 1st Army fighting fiercely to drive them out.

PLUTO

The Americans had laid an overland pipeline from Le Havre to take fuel arriving by sea from the States to bring it up to the advancing troops. In due course, large tankers would be brought into Antwerp and smaller tankers into

Mobile
laundry.

PLUTO pipeline. (RLC Museum)

PLUTO pipeline. (RLC Museum)

other ports along the French Channel coast. Nevertheless, the needs of the advancing army were such that the PLUTO supplies would still be needed.

The Dungeness pipeline had not been planned to flow until the armies had advanced sufficiently. It too had met with problems. The first pipeline was laid on 27 October and this was followed by four more, although it was reported that only 62,000 tons of petrol had actually reached France by the end of January. Revisions were made, which in effect meant that the two types of pipe were combined, with the more flexible used at the shore end. In the months up to the German surrender up to 1 million gallons per day flowed through the seventeen pipelines then in place.[14]

OPERATION MARKET GARDEN

The time taken to get from Normandy to Antwerp had tested the patience of the politicians and so, unbeknown to the troops on the ground, Field Marshal Montgomery had conceived a plan to strike quickly into the heart of Germany. This was codenamed Operation Market Garden and would

take place on 17 September. It was to be a massive airborne attack. Airborne divisions would take the bridges at Eindhoven and Nijmegen, and General Horrocks' 30 Corps would advance down to take Arnhem and then drive into industrial Germany.

Among those who would take off from RAF Barkston Heath, in Lincolnshire, for Arnhem were men of the RAOC,[15] some of whom formed the ordnance field park recce party whose job it was to seek out large garages and commandeer suitable vehicles to help transport the troops from the drop points. It was a group of seven men, including Private Ted Mordecai, who wrote an account of the five days he spent face to face with the enemy.

The beginning was so positive. The Dutch civilians, all wearing marigolds, welcomed the British soldiers landing near Arnhem as saviours. A small village pub offered beer, which they had been told to refuse. Local people gave them cups of ersatz (substitute) coffee. With the news that the battalion ahead of them was encountering tough opposition, they were ordered to press forward at all speed.

Further orders came that their intended role had been shelved and they were to take an active part in securing the bridge across the river. Ted's words paint the picture:

> As we moved up the road parallel to the river we could see the span bridge outlined against flashes of gunfire against the sky. At the same time the Germans on the other side of the river were concentrating all their fire in our direction and at the bridge ... the sound of shot and shell was deafening, but we inched our way forward up to the bridge.

They successfully occupied a house within reach of the bridge. It was 2000 hours on 17 September:

> Shortly after daybreak we heard the sound of engines revving up and, looking towards the other side of the bridge to the South, we saw a line of open topped 'Opel' armoured cars coming across the bridge in line astern ... one of our six pounder anti-tank guns caught the first car in the middle, and it slewed round and blocked the bridge ... everyone within range opened fire at the cars with Brens, Stens, rifles and grenades.

Once quiet descended, Captain Manley suggested that everyone should try to get some sleep. Mordecai received a rude awakening from a loud explosion:

We couldn't believe our eyes at what we saw. Either a mortar bomb or 88mm shell had hit the back of the house and there was a gaping hole where the back wall and the roof should have been.

They took cover in the cellar of the house and remained hidden until the sporadic firing stopped:

We were ordered back upstairs and resumed our position at the windows … we heard a klaxon horn and whistles sounding at odd intervals … in the afternoon we saw some Spitfires patrolling over the town and, hearing the sound of heavier engines, we guessed that the lift timed for Monday was taking place.

Towards evening, just as the sun was dipping down, we heard our old battle cry of 'Whahoo M****!' ring out and going out onto the veranda just in front of the bedroom windows we waved our green recognition silks which we wore as scarves and returned the battle cry, thinking reinforcements had arrived. Our elation was short lived as they turned out only to be a small platoon with a six pounder.

A town house close by had been hit and 'was blazing like an inferno and lit up the surrounding area'.

Tuesday dawned with a hint of fine weather and about 0800 hours we decided that it was time for a 'brew-up' … no water was forthcoming and suddenly we heard a whistling sound … an explosion followed almost immediately. We lay on the floor whilst splinters of steel came whanging through the window and hitting the outside wall.

Captain Manley told us that 30 Corps under General Horrocks had been held up by enemy opposition and it would be some time before they reached us.

We could hear tracks clanking away on the road. We all hugged the ground not daring to lift our faces in case some German spotted us. The clanking sound came nearer and, lifting my head slightly, I could see the dark shape of the tank through the hedge about ten feet away. The tank slowly moved off … we made a mad dash across the road to the demolished houses near the bridge. On our way across we were silhouetted against the flames from the houses we had vacated earlier and a German machine gunner must have spotted us as he opened fire on us and tracer bullets came through the darkness in our direction.

Other guns opened fire:

This fire was so concentrated it kept us pinned down for what seemed ages … during a lull I said to Harry, 'We aren't going to be relieved and I think we should swim across the river and make our way to our own lines.' Harry replied, 'I think we should stay together and hope for the best.'

It was now quite obvious we were on our own and cut off, as the deadline for being relieved had passed some hours earlier … we were completely hemmed in and gradually being compressed into an ever decreasing circle.

Ted Mordecai and his small unit went from house to house seeking safety from the Germans, who were now preparing for a final onslaught; at the same time, they took every opportunity themselves to attack and cause the maximum damage. Ted got separated from his mates and found himself at Brigade HQ. The senior officer gave him a bottle of wine and encouraged him to rest. He continued his account:

I heard someone shouting, 'does anybody here know anything about Bren guns?' The shouting went on and so I went into a front room covering the street and told an officer that [being RAOC] I knew something about Brens. There was a gunner manning the Bren gun in the window with a corporal acting as his No 2. The gunner said he couldn't fire the Bren as it wouldn't work. I moved into his position and tried the standard procedure of removing the magazine, cocking the gun and squeezing the trigger. I told the corporal that the gun was OK and put the magazine back in and squeezed the trigger. It didn't work as the bolt would not push the cartridge into the barrel. So, removing the magazine, I ejected two of the cartridges, put the magazine back in the gun and tried again. This time it fired. Whoever had loaded the magazine had crammed too many cartridges in it, consequently they were too tight to move. Although the magazine would hold 32 cartridges, it was policy never to put in more than 28. The officer asked me if I would take over the gun. I therefore became the Bren gunner of the last bastion.

Ted manned the gun until the ammunition ran out and he then reverted to his Sten, like the others. The mad dashes from one house to the next continued as the Germans followed, demolishing houses with the fire of 88mm guns:

There was a lull in proceedings and it was during this period that Jerry called upon us to surrender and a truce was called whilst a discussion took place between the Germans and our officers who were left. The truce lasted about an hour during which time Jerry agreed to let us hand over our wounded. After the wounded had been evacuated the Germans again called upon us to surrender as we were completely cut off, surrounded and nearly out of ammunition. Jerry was told in Army fashion to 'Shove off' but much cruder and when someone threw a grenade at them hostilities commenced once again.

The shelling continued:

I felt a blow like being hit with a stick on the right side of my face and across my right eye as the blast whipped under my helmet. It lifted me off my feet and knocked me flat out and when I came round I couldn't see a thing. Eventually I could make out things in the darkness with my left eye, but all I could see out of my right eye was a blinding glare. I felt my face but couldn't feel any blood and, as the shelling was still taking place, decided to try to find some cover. I crawled over the ground and eventually found a slit trench up against the wall and flopped in on top of another chap lying in the bottom. The shelling kept on all night and there was no reply from any of our chaps at all. They were either lying low or there weren't any left.

Dawn eventually came and everything was very quiet … the chap under me stirred and said he was going to surrender … I stood up in the trench and the first thing that met my sight [through my left eye] was an 88mm shell with a bent nose lying half over the edge of the trench … being careful not to disturb it I climbed out … I waited a while, but couldn't hear any shooting and so decided to give myself up.

When night fell, a small group of us, being walking wounded, were herded into the back of a small truck and transported to hospital.

Later I volunteered to help out one of our MOs … it opened my eyes to the aftermath of battle as I was assisting in an amputees ward which had both German and British patients. Another thing that brought home the horrors of war was seeing a pile of discarded odd boots where they had been thrown after legs had been amputated.

As Jerry had said, 'For you Tommy, the war is over.'

Stan Carter had returned to France on 8 August and his unit had been held up at Arnhem. He joined 17 BAD and recalled running out of supplies as a result of the sheer length of the line of communication.[16]

The failure of Operation Market Garden placed an increased urgency on the ordnance team in Antwerp. The advance into Germany would be long and gruelling and would demand substantial supplies, including replacing the losses 30 Corps had suffered.

ANTWERP AND ON TO THE RHINE

During October, the Antwerp Depot combined 15 AOD with both 17 and 16 AOD as they relinquished their site in Normandy, and by 1 November the first trickle of stores from England began to arrive.[17] The impact was massive, replacing the 300-mile drive from Normandy and largely beach landings with a port, a relatively simple sea journey and a very much shorter journey to where the troops were fighting.

In early 1945, Colonel Bob Hiam, who had been commanding 14 AOD, took over from Colonel Volkers, who was posted out to the Far East to continue preparations for the anticipated equally gruelling land war against Japan. The new base was vast. In November 1944, 3,900 military and civilians had set to work to get storehouses and offices ready. In April, some 13,000 were employed, most of whom were civilian. Under German occupation, many English-speaking Belgians had been unable to obtain work; now they relished the opportunity provided by the AOD.

The AOD was broken down into depots for motor transport, general stores including clothing, and technical stores including armaments and signals. In addition a stores transit depot was set up in Bruges to receive supplies ordered by units from the UK. There were two returned stores units, processing 25,000 tons a month.

With the move to Antwerp, the Main Base Stores Transit Depot, which had been at Micheldever on the London–Winchester–Southampton line since D-Day, was moved to Stratford in East London and this supplied stores to a coaster, a dedicated ship which ferried stores across the Channel, initially to Normandy, then Dieppe and Ostend, but now to Antwerp. More urgent items came by air from Northolt.

For the advance into Germany, FTSs were set up for each of the 2nd Army, the Canadian Army, the Army Base Workshops and for the units forming the lines of communication between the AOD and the fighting unit. The vehicle companies were now to come into their own as the lifeblood of the advancing army.

Following hospitalisation, infantry man George Forster was posted to 16 Vehicle Company HQ in Brussels. His particular role was in the

DUKW crossing the Rhine. (RLC Museum)

quartermaster stores of the company, where he would issue replacement boots and uniforms to company personnel.

Three other factors would have a major impact before the final thrust into Germany could be made. In the south of France troops were arriving from Italy and North Africa. These were making their way by road and rail to Paris and then joining General Patton and the US Army as it advanced north-east towards Germany. These troops needed to be equipped.

The next factor was, once again, the weather. It first froze, and the lying snow demanded winter clothing for the troops and also a different camouflage. These were provided just as the thaw set in. Now it was water and mud that had to be fought. Here, the reserve of DUKWs and other amphibious vehicles came into their own, as did those vehicles in reserve that were still with their waterproofing.

The third factor was very much of the Germans' making and was the surprise counter-attack on the Americans in the Ardennes. The drive through by the Panzers was costly in terms of American tanks. The US Army naturally looked to the RAOC, who held hundreds of Shermans in reserve ready to replace losses from the British armoured divisions. Many of these were quickly redirected to the Americans once British radios had been replaced with American equipment. The 21st Army Group was thus ready to press ahead to the Rhine.

As a precursor to the crossing itself (Operation Plunder), Operation Veritable[18] demanded support from some ten ordnance field parks in order to move up to the western bank of the Rhine. Operation Plunder was an amphibious and airborne attack as complex as D-Day itself. Ordnance was called upon to produce Asdic echo-sounding apparatus, fluorescent tapes and panels, light floats (smoke producing flares), land mattresses (artillery shells), Tabby (night vision) equipment, Mae Wests (life preservers), Weasels (snow vehicles), Windsor carriers (Canadian longer version of the Bren carrier) and other specialist equipment, all of which needed their own spare parts.

The concentration of troops into marshalling areas began on 20 March. A heavy smokescreen was demanded and at 2100 hours on 23 March the crossing began. Stores followed in the early hours of 24 March. The 11th Armoured Division[19] had been supplied with new tanks and discovered the factory-fitted fan belts were faulty and so 200 new fan belts were needed in forty-eight hours unless the advance was to be halted. The senior ordnance officer of 8 Corps sent for replacements and these were despatched from Old Dalby and flown out ready to be fitted with no resulting delay. The 2nd Army was thus ready to break out into the heart of Germany supported by FTSs.

BELSEN

On 15 April, 8 Corps arrived at Belsen and the Deputy Director of Ordnance Services 8 Corps was one of the first to enter the camp.[20] The camp, he found, was:

… a cesspit of filth and disease; men, women and children were dying by the hundred every day; and 10,000 unburied bodies, in various stages of decomposition lay around. Priority one was to get the medical services going, and within 48 hours, 304 mobile laundry was in the camp and working. Bath sections 304, 105, 305 and 310 Mobile laundries arrived within a matter of days. and inmates of the camp were soon having their first bath since imprisonment.

On entry into the camp the medical teams found that of 28,135 women, 21,000 required hospitalisation and of 12,000 men over 9,000 required urgent treatment from conditions including typhus, tuberculosis, enteritis and famine oedema. The most immediate tasks were the burial of the dead, the washing of the living and the provision of clothing, and the dusting of everything to kill lice.

Requisitions of clothing had been made from the local population and substantial stores were discovered in the blocks previously occupied by SS guards. These stores, including clothing and bedding, were issued to non-hospitalised inmates. The block itself was converted into use as a hospital and again much of the equipment needed was found to have been on site. The remaining equipment needed was brought in by ordnance personnel from the Antwerp AOD. The operation, led by 249 (Oxfordshire Yeomanry) Battery of 53 Anti-Tank Regiment, included, in addition to RAOC personnel operating baths and laundries, men from REME, RASC, Military Government and, of course, the British Red Cross and RAMC General Hospital, Field Hygiene, Light Field Ambulance and Mobile Bacteriological Laboratory.

In spite of everything that was being done, the death toll continued to be high for many days.

THE ADVANCE INTO GERMANY

After the crossing of the Rhine, the advance into Germany was swift and few casualties were suffered. John Frost[21] recalled the horrific war damage, seeing every building 'smashed to smithereens, villagers holding out white flags, apprehensive and frightened'.

It was at this point that many old Cruiser and Crusader tanks came into their own. With a particular attachment they became Centaur bulldozers and performed essential work in clearing the way through bombed German towns, as this message from the Ministry of Supply indicates: 'Your effort on Centaur bulldozers has been absolutely magnificent and fully justifies waving the flag. The reports we have had on Centaur bulldozer after crossing the Rhine have been first-class and indicate the effort was well worth while.'[22]

On 8 May 1945 the Germans capitulated. The 21st Army Group now became an army of occupation and the task of clearing up fell to ordnance. The *Daily Telegraph* of 19 September 1945[23] carried a piece entitled, 'Rapid British Clearance of Nazi War Material':

The greatest mopping up operation in history is taking place in Germany and we are seeing some astonishing things. Guns, tanks, vehicles and fantastically large quantities of other materials are being collected and sorted throughout the Reich … two big tasks are being undertaken simultaneously: The Allies are steadily gathering their own property; they are taking away from the Germans every war-like article they possess.

The article goes on to explain that demobilisation of experienced technical personnel was being delayed to ensure that the right people were on hand. These RAOC men had undergone special training prior to the invasion in order to be ready for the dismantling of the German war organisation. The article then quotes an experienced RAOC officer who had seen it all before:

As a member of the Control Commission that was set up in Germany after the 1914 war, I cannot help noticing the very different conditions in which I have worked with the Control Commission of today. The trouble on the last occasion was that we occupied only a small part of Germany and were handicapped at every turn. Today the position is different. The control we exercise is complete and the Germans have not been given any chance to practise evasion. We have gone through their territory like locusts and stripped it bare. We have dealt with everything that matters and their chances of repeating the tactics of a generation ago are hopeless. We have already accomplished more than in five years at the end of the 1914 war. At the same time, we are accomplishing something equally important by salving a vast mass of our own material. Obviously we cannot hope to get back what we spent on it, but the methods we have followed will certainly prove of distinct benefit to the taxpayer.

It was an operation that would take many months. Ken Brown[24] transferred to the RAOC from the Gunners after VE day 'because the pay was better', and was posted to Germany to work on the destruction of the German stores of ammunition. 'They would pile up all but the largest shells, cover with petrol, stand well back and set alight – it was like starting many small wars.'

It wasn't just in Germany, Rhei Williams[25] was wounded following his landing on Juno Beach and was then invalided back to England. After a period in hospital he was posted to Old Dalby and given the job of identifying returned spare parts using his former skills as a motor mechanic. He remembered working alongside a number of other wounded or old soldiers as well as civilians and young recruits.

The war in Europe may have been won, but all but a very small select group of American military and politicians believed that there would now be a far more gruelling land war against Japan.

THE FAR EAST

The Far East was another part of the world where the presence of Army Ordnance transparently ran hand-in-hand with the British Empire; wherever there was Empire there were soldiers, in largely policing roles, and wherever there were soldiers there were armaments, the meat and drink of ordnance.

It is therefore not surprising that officers and men of the RAOC were to be found in such places as Hong Kong and Singapore, that parallel organisations were to be found in the shape of the Indian and Australian Ordnance Corps or that there should be a photograph of RAOC officers and men in Shanghai in 1925 in the RAOC archives. In a sense, this was a very different RAOC to that found in the stores sheds of Chilwell or Didcot; nevertheless, it was the self-same organisation, facing essentially the same challenges.

In 1937 a new ordnance depot, the Alexandra Depot, had been built near the docks in Singapore. Captain J.G. Denniston, who later had such a

View of BOD Singapore.

BOD Singapore as left by the Japanese.

pivotal role in the 21st Army Group, had had the foresight to insist on space for expansion. This was used as Singapore moved from peacetime to a war footing. In December 1941 there were some 60,000 troops stationed there, with an RAOC compliment of nine officers and 140 other ranks. There were also units of Australian and Indian Ordnance. There were advance depots on the Malay Peninsula and an ordnance field park in Thailand. Some 1,500 vehicles were held at the BOD.[1]

Hong Kong was seen as less strategic and there were some 12,000 troops and an RAOC complement of fifteen officers and 132 other ranks on the island.[2]

THE DEFENCE AND SURRENDER OF SINGAPORE

In early December 1941 the 400-strong 4th Ordnance Stores Company was forming at Deepcut as the ordnance element of the 18th Division. Men had come from depots around the country.

Douglas Hanson,[3] a motor mechanic, had escaped death on the sinking of the *Lancastria*, but had suffered serious burns. He came to Aldershot on

VRS convoy for Hong Kong.

release from convalescence. Frank Newton came from the food industry and had been called up just as he was planning his wedding. He had been posted to COD Branston and had spent his first few months stacking and sorting bales of cloth. Others in the company were drivers, radio mechanics, bootmakers and men skilled with ammunition and armaments.

Their intended destination was the Middle East. In the event, they docked at Durban and changed ships to one bound for Singapore. The events of 7 December 1941 in the Pacific had changed everything, and for Douglas and his fellow ordnance men the priority became the defence of Singapore.

An account written in the Changi Prisoner-of-War Camp on 6 March 1942[4] tells the story of the defeat and surrender at Singapore and how ordnance men played their part in what was called the Alexandra Defence Force. Douglas Hanson[5] recalled nearing the Sunda Straits on the approach to Singapore and the terror of being dive-bombed. He and the rest of 4th Ordnance Store Company landed on 5 February, ten days before the surrender to the Japanese. He recalled the atmosphere growing steadily worse, with no naval or air defence. Eventually the Japanese captured the water supply and surrender followed. Among his colleagues in the RAOC there was a sense of relief, since being only recently declared 'combatant' they had, as yet, neither the equipment nor training to take on jungle-toughened troops.

THE DEFENCE AND SURRENDER OF HONG KONG

The main ordnance stores on Hong Kong were either side of Queen's Road, by the docks. There was considerable ammunition held on three sites, workshops at Shousson Hill and other stores on sites around the island including, importantly, on the Ridge. The COO was Lieutenant Colonel Macpherson who had transferred from the Royal Scots before the war. The total garrison was commanded by Major General Maltby and included a large Canadian contingent.

Lance Corporal Charles Colebrook[6] worked in the ordnance workshop, having been transferred from the Royal Engineers. The Japanese directed their attention to Hong Kong almost immediately after Pearl Harbor and Charles Colebrook was in the thick of it. His expertise with searchlights had him sent to Kowloon to repair anti-aircraft lights being operated by an Indian regiment who had no repair know-how. He remembered being issued with a brand new Hillman and taking the ferry to Kowloon loaded up with tools and spare parts.

Hillman Tilly. (RLC Museum)

In the event, he repaired one searchlight and replaced another. Returning to the island under fire he then helped to ferry stores away from Queen's Road up to the Ridge. This was followed by a series of moves by the men of the ordnance unit to try to resist the advancing Japanese. Most of this centred on the Ridge and they experienced heavy fire, with many killed and wounded.

At one point the party divided into four, with one heading for Repulse Bay. This party was ambushed and all but Captain Ebbage and his sergeant major were killed. The remaining party was attacked head-on and Colebrook, manning the Bren gun, admitted that he was 'afraid he got a few'. Soon after, the order came through to surrender. The Japanese refused to accept it, and Colebrook thought this was because of the casualties they had suffered. It was later found that, of some fifty left behind to defend the Ridge, none survived.

Colebrook's party then decided to get through to Repulse Bay but found the Japanese already there with their flag flying from the hotel. His group finally managed to surrender on 24 December with the island as a whole surrendering on Christmas Day.

PRISONERS OF WAR

The Far East was where a great many RAOC POWs were taken, although many were also taken in the BEF, Greece and Crete. I offer the following accounts of life as POWs as a tribute to those who didn't survive or who didn't record their experience, and with thanks to those who did.

Captivity for Charles Colebrook and his fellow prisoners from Hong Kong came first with soldiers, civilians, men, women and children being herded together at North Point. The soldiers were then separated and sent to Shamshipu Camp. Here, Colebrook volunteered for the hospital set up for diphtheria patients who arrived with captured Canadians. He was there for a year and nursed prisoners suffering from both diphtheria and dysentery.

Having quite remarkably survived, Captain Ebbage sent for him and, to fill the required quota of prisoners, he was sent to a camp near Nagasaki, where he worked with a group of electricians in a factory dismantling rotors. Here they endured earthquakes and floods and daily bombing by the Americans. They were told by the camp commandant 'not to feel happy because Japan was being bombed', and junior soldiers were given free rein to take out their anger on the prisoners just as the more senior soldiers took it out on them. Colebrook remembers POWs arriving from Singapore having worked on the railway and saying they wished themselves back there rather than having to endure the brutality of this camp. Colebrook and his fellow prisoners suffered the severe ill effects of malnutrition in the same way as others had in Thailand.

Colebrook's unit was moved to a factory some 5 miles from Hiroshima. He remembered the sound of rumbling through the hills when the A bomb was dropped; he believes it was the favourable wind direction that saved him. Shortly afterwards they were taken by train through Hiroshima and witnessed its total destruction. When he volunteered to help the wounded in a Japanese hospital, he witnessed the great many civilians suffering from severe burns. He was repatriated to San Francisco, then by rail to New York and finally on the *Queen Mary* to England. He never fully recovered.

Douglas Hanson[7] recalled the Japanese being overwhelmed by the number of troops who had surrendered and how they essentially left them in the command of their own officers to make their way to Changi Village and Camp. He recalled five days when the Singapore garrison was unmanned as the Japanese Navy took over from the army. Nevertheless, at that point escape seemed unrealistic. He and his fellow prisoners grew steadily weaker on their diet of polished rice, robbed of essential vitamin B which had been extracted for the Japanese troops to protect them against beri-beri.

Frank Newton's account[8] confirmed Hanson's view that the Japanese were overwhelmed by their numbers and that the British were largely left to themselves, or seemed to be. His memory was of being sent to hunt for ordnance stores, particularly tents and clothing (the Branston type of store). With what they found they erected their own camp, set up a quartermasters store for clothing, and set boot repairers (a trade ever present in RAOC stores companies) to work.

Slowly, the Japanese became more organised and a first crisis came when the POWs were ordered to sign a document agreeing not to try to escape.

The mass refusal that met this led to reprisals that were only eased when the general commanding the British forces issued an order exempting those who signed from court martial. Frank soon became ill and spent long periods in hospital, where he was generally well looked after. In the periods in between he was assigned light duties. He recalled being required to strip down scrapped engines, but managing at the same time to make them incapable of operation. He and his fellow prisoners built and maintained the camps where they were held and cooked such food as there was. He was in hospital when the Allies arrived in 1945.

Stanley Dawson[9] may have been part of the original garrison, or a new arrival like Hanson and Newton. His experience as a POW in Thailand was very much worse, as he and thousands of other British, Australian and Dutch POWs laboured on the railway. His account is of deprivation, illness and almost institutionalised cruelty, although a report in the war crimes court pointed more at barbaric individuals than the army as a whole.

He and those with him were set to heavy manual work on building the railway through Thailand. This type of work had claimed the lives of many Irish navvies building the railways in nineteenth-century England. They too had been forced to work harder than the human body can stand; they too were malnourished and lived in conditions that beggared belief. Dawson wrote of having to work through the day and well into the night and having neither the time nor energy to go down to the ice-cold river to wash while being bitten by countless mosquitos, nor to remove the countless bedbugs that took occupation of the 2ft by 6ft of bamboo that acted as a bed. Many would opt to sleep on the bare earth ravaged by mosquitos rather than endure a sleepless night of those bugs.

As a group of ordnance men, there were drivers in Dawson's camp and these were ordered by the Japanese to drive their transport. There were also radio mechanics. He recounted how some of these secreted radio parts gathered with other stores in Singapore. These parts were made into radio sets, which were hidden and provided a much needed stream of news of the war. Radios need batteries, and a system was developed whereby the batteries of Japanese lorries driven by RAOC prisoners would be removed and replaced with used batteries and then secreted for later use. When these radios were found, as they inevitably were, the makers were subjected to horrific beatings that were so bad they made them cry out for mercy.

Amid this horror there was still, as with Frank Newton, the daily round. The camp was maintained and food cooked. Sickness was rife, with beri-beri that made work and walking neigh impossible, malaria, dysentery, leg ulcers through to the bone, scabies and cholera, which took a regular toll of POWs.

Cholera was the only disease that the Japanese took seriously, given the danger it held for everyone.

Cigarettes were paid for from the 25 cents a day that working POWs were given. There was trade with the local population but always at the risk of reprisals. Religious worship was allowed. On Easter Day 1943 the first letters from home arrived, some had been posted the previous July.

There were other moments of respite. On occasional breaks from work we were content to savour the glories of the tropical night – the air still and cool – and watch the moon magically transform the bamboo thickets into silver groves'. Moving from one work project to the next brought extreme challenges. If travelling by rail, days would be spent standing crammed in wagons, and if on foot, there was the pain of marching in the heat and the potentially fatal risk of drinking any water found.

An account of his experience as a prisoner of the Japanese was provided by P.R. Barroud[10] along with a copy of a letter written by the senior RAOC officer to an alderman of his home town. The letter, signed by Charles Graham Steadman, reported:

> Myself and fifty other RAOC personnel of the 18th Division moved into Thailand about 18 months ago. Many others have followed including Officers and men of No 14 Section, 4th Ordnance Stores Company, Indian Army Ordnance Corps, 18th Division Field Park, 18th Divisional Workshops, Light Aid Detachments and unit attached personnel … We built this camp which is situated on the banks of a river. It is quite a large settlement, the building comprising bamboo and attar structures.

The letter went on to tell of the high morale and generally good conditions enjoyed. Importantly, at the beginning it was at pains to stress that the letter had been sanctioned by the Imperial Japanese Army and was intended to inform families of the welfare and life led by POWs. Significantly, the letter was written on the back of a blank declaration in both English and Japanese that the undersigned 'hereby solemnly swears on my honour that I will not, under any circumstances, attempt escape'.

Lance Corporal Barroud's papers contained sketches of motor car designs and also the layout of a workshop: perhaps his dreams while incarcerated. They also contained a diary which began at Hedge End Camp at Luggershall, Hampshire, on 28 September 1939 and showed that he had served with an ordnance LAD with the Royal Artillery. He was, by trade, an automobile engineer and became an armaments artificer. Also in the papers was a roll of the names of survivors at Pratchai POW camp in Siam. He was awarded the 1939–45 Star for service in the BEF, from 29 September 1939 to 2 June 1940, from which we can infer that he was evacuated at Dunkirk. He was awarded the Pacific Star for service in Malaya, from 28 October 1941 until he became a POW on the surrender of Singapore on 15 February 1942. He was thus probably a member of the garrison and the original Alexandria Defence Force.

Some records suggest that Lieutenant Colonel C.H. McVittie[11] had been sent up the peninsula to face the advancing Japanese. His own account of his imprisonment as a POW confirms that he was with the RAOC units in Singapore. I remember Major General McVittie when he and his wife would visit my father and mother after McVittie had stepped into my father's shoes as COS in the late 1950s. I remember most the hushed respect granted to him as a former Japanese POW, in my boyish eyes confirmed by films such as the *Bridge Over the River Kwai*.

McVittie's account of his four and a half years is different. Astonishingly he was not one of the many sent to work on the railway; he stayed in or around Changi and Singapore for the duration. His concern, like the hero in the Kwai, was to keep soldiers, soldiers. His account began with these chilling words:

> It all began on Sunday 15th February 1942 at 6.00pm when Gen Percival ordered the 'cease-fire' as a prelude to the unconditional surrender of the Singapore Fortress to the Nippon Army. In my opinion one of the most terrible pages in British History which will not be written in its true perspective in our time.

Like the other Singapore prisoners, McVittie recalled the business-as-usual nature of the first months of captivity. He recalled the incident with the declaration that prisoners had to sign, and remembered periods of severe overcrowding. He recalled the parties sent up-country, amazed that he was never selected. He recalled the return of a fraction of the number that had been sent and the dreadful condition they were in. He recalled the deterioration in the nutritional value of the food they were given and the way men would do anything to improve their diet.

He told how quickly soldiers lost their self-discipline and how difficult this was to rebuild in the squalid conditions in which they had to live. He emphasised the importance of work and study, even when the officers were made to labour along with their men. One of his greatest fears was to be without work.

It is more than possible that his somewhat anodyne account was influenced by the knowledge that it would be censored. In the main body of the handwritten account there are phrases and sentences that have been obliterated.

PREPARATIONS FOR A LAND WAR AGAINST JAPAN

The Japanese effectively controlled the Bay of Bengal until late 1943, from when the 14th Army engaged them in the jungles of Burma. The provision of supplies was extremely demanding and dangerous, but effected in collaboration with the RAF, principally 31 Squadron, who either dropped supplies or flew in and out of clearings. Indian Ordnance had set up ordnance field depots, advance ordnance depots and advance ammunition depots to support the North-West Frontier with Burma. However, severe problems were being experienced with delays and the state in which stores arrived.

Bill Williams was sent out to via the Middle East to India and Burma in October–December 1943 to investigate and report.[12] The North African bases were already very well established but also very well stocked, and probably overstocked, given that the only conflict then under way was in Italy. The issue was to see how the North African machine could be brought into play in Italy, but also in India. While the Allies had agreed that the invasion of northern Europe should be the priority, there was a war to be fought against Japan and that would need careful but different attention from an ordnance point of view.

The core issues were the old chestnuts of spare parts and packaging, but in the context of the Far East these became much sharper, with a hostile climate, a vast area and much activity expected in impenetrable jungle. The base from which the British would advance was India. As a long-established base of Empire, it already had depots of the Indian Ordnance Corps, but these were thinly spread and geared only to a peacetime role.

The visit to India resulted in a report from which a number of key themes can be identified. There was a shortage of spare parts worldwide. The experience in North Africa was that shortages occurred as a result of spares being hoarded, when surplus spares should have been returned to central depots. The report was silent on the subject of pilfering.

Another source of shortage was the result of inadequate and inappropriate packaging. India would be encouraged to take on the new packing methods rolled out in the US and elsewhere. A third source resulted from the dispersal of motor vehicle and technical spares to commands so that they were spread too thinly and this led to the low likelihood that the right spare would be at the right command depot. Bill recommended that such spares should be concentrated in two major depots – Calcutta for general stores and Madras for vehicle spares and technical stores.

The Indian Army was stretched, from a manpower point of view. Perceived shortages in Indian ordnance had been addressed by the transfer of surplus inexperienced officers from elsewhere in the army. Bill stressed that ordnance needed men with business experience, who were good man-managers and well organised. One solution was using more civilian staff, but if this was to be achieved pay rates would need to be increased in order to be competitive and provision would need to be made for housing staff near to depots or failing that, better transport from residential areas. The office of the Indian director of ordnance was also too thinly staffed to be effective. He offered to send some key officers from the UK.

Although Bill had shied away from mechanical accounting, he was entirely clear that a modern army needed proper telephones, record-keeping and office equipment, and stores needed proper storage equipment. He recommended that this should be supplied, especially to the key depots.

A major issue was highlighted when Bill was invited by the commander-in-chief in India, General Sir Claude Auchinleck, to address a large audience of officers in Delhi. He stressed the vital importance of keeping senior ordnance officers 'fully in the operational picture so that they can anticipate the requirements for Ordnance stores and ammunition'.

The report had a number of significant impacts. Two key officers were sent out from Britain. Colonel Browne with his experience of technical stores was sent from Greenford to become commandant of 206 Indian Base Ordnance Depot, and Lieutenant Colonel Stan Preston was sent from Feltham with a wealth of experience of packing MT spares for the tropics. Preston became deputy commandant.

In looking at South East Asia Command, COD Feltham was a crucial part of the picture. The packing of spares was a recurring issue and one that became much sharper with the hot and damp climate. This was tackled by a joint initiative of US and British Ordnance and was revealed in a major packaging exhibition at Feltham in 1944.[13] The booklet accompanying the exhibition identified five 'Allies of the Japs':

Distance: stores need to move thousands of miles with as many as twenty transhipments for one campaign. This means that, with inevitable rough handling, stores arrive broken; en route they are vulnerable to enemy attack; at any one time stores fill the supply chain from home to the theatre of war, meaning that the majority is not in use.

Climate: 100 degrees in the shade; 165 in the sun; 80 to 90% humidity; more rain in one typhoon than in a year in southern England; gales 50% greater than the worst Atlantic storms. Packaging gets soaked, labels wash away, steel rusts badly overnight, aluminium and plastics corrode, mirrors decompose and rubber rots.

Terrains: paddy fields with a foot of water over two feet of mud; all over except high mountains there is jungle. Stores packed too heavily or awkwardly will be left behind. Lighter weights are necessary in hot humid climates.

Jungle pests: fungi grow quickly, rot and destroy; insects grow monstrous, rats are bold, bacteria thrive; where one cannot get, another will penetrate. Fungi make wireless sets useless, bacteria even form on optical instruments.

Environment: lasting acclimatisation in the humid tropics is almost impossible. Task must be made as simple as possible.

The booklet went on to show just how much had been lost because of inadequate packaging. The answer was a comprehensive approach built round three words: Preservation – Identification – Packaging (PIP). The range of stores to be subjected to this process was simply vast:

Tanks and engines (350,000 different items)
Engineering (60,000)
Armaments and small arms (75,000)
Aircraft (750,000)
Clothing and stores (60,000)
Signals and radar (80,000)
Food (400)
Medical supplies (30,000)

It is interesting that, after five years of war, not only were the Allies working together but so were services, with the inclusion of aircraft parts. The work was not just undertaken by ordnance, the controller of chemical research and development provided a report on 'tropic proofing'. One result of all this was the issue of a comprehensive booklet entitled *Tropical*

ATS personnel in COD Feltham stores.

Packaging, but there were also detailed regulations on tropical storage.

The *Motor Trader* magazine of 27 December 1944[14] brought its focus on to PIP – the Preservation, Identification and Packaging of stores:

> For the war in the Pacific a new set of problems had to be tackled. War materials in the Far East have to be packed in a very different way. Waterproofing is called upon in nearly every instance and a special production technique of tropic proofing is called upon from suppliers. Taking a piston, for example, first clean it; second coat it in preservative; to protect the preservative wrap it up in corrugated paper; label it and then put it in a carton which in turn must have a label; the carton is next wrapped, immersed in a sealing solution and a label put on the sealed carton; finally, the label must be sprayed with a protective solution so it will not smudge or peel off.

In March 1944 the Japanese attacked from Burma and broke through the Indian border. Fierce resistance by the 14th Army and General William Slim drove them back but kept thousands of Japanese engaged, allowing the Americans to make progress in the Pacific. The 14th Army was desperate for spare parts to enable it to keep advancing, and for a full land attack on Japan even more supplies would be needed.

Bill Williams made a further visit to the Middle East (PAIC, Persian and Iraq Command) and East Africa in November and December 1944.[15] The purpose this time was rationalisation. If spare parts and supplies were

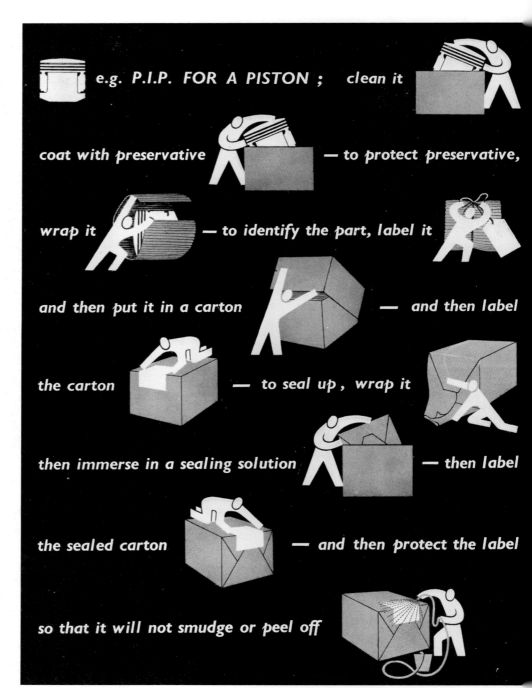

'Far East Packing Methods' poster.

COD Feltham packaging exhibition.

limited, then every effort needed to be made to ensure that they were made available where they were needed.

The report on the visit highlights just how worrying the prospect of a land war with Japan had become. The war with Germany was over, but the clear expectation was that the conflict with Japan would take years and tons of equipment and would demand good people.

Bill visited India again in March 1945,[16] going in particular to 206 IBOD. The focus was on Allied Land Forces South East Asia (ALFSEA). The base depot itself seemed to be operating effectively, but for the remainder of the report many of the recommendations in the 1943 report were repeated. Among the rather telling comments was this:

Tropicalised packing has now reached such a level of perfection in the U.K. and America that it is tragic if current receipts are broken open and the special tropicalisation destroyed merely for the purpose of carrying out inspections in Central Depots in India.

There seems to be an echo of the problems Donnington had experienced with Russian inspections.

Nevertheless, the push from India through Burma was going to require effective supply and Bill must have returned home unconvinced that this would be the case. He appointed a new DOS for India and promised more postings of good officers from UK depots.

In the summer of 1945 plans were progressing for an invasion of Malaya and LRs and BMPs were being prepared at 206 IBOD. In support of this effort, Bill made a further visit to Canada and the US. The first issue addressed was a serious hold-up in supply of spare parts for jeeps sent to India and SEAC. Most of the jeeps that had been sent were reconditioned vehicles from the European theatre. Bill stressed the need for spares for LRs, BMPs and for the AOD that would be set up following an invasion. The US War Department made arrangements immediately to meet the request. At subsequent visits, a key point was how limited raw materials for waterproofing could be divided between the Americans and British.

Plans were clearly under way for the invasion of Pacific islands. Bill inspected Ford-manufactured amphibious vehicles, both with mounted guns and for the transport of men and equipment. An interesting almost postscript to many of the meetings was the planning for the continued use of depots after hostilities ceased. There was no evidence of an expectation that activity would return to the former peacetime levels. The final meeting of the trip, at the large Longue Pointe Depot, really began to grasp the huge nettle of the clean-up after the war, cancellation orders for equipment and just how to deal with the vast quantities that would be held worldwide.

In the event, the dropping of the nuclear bomb made this abortive.

'Packing for the Far East' poster.

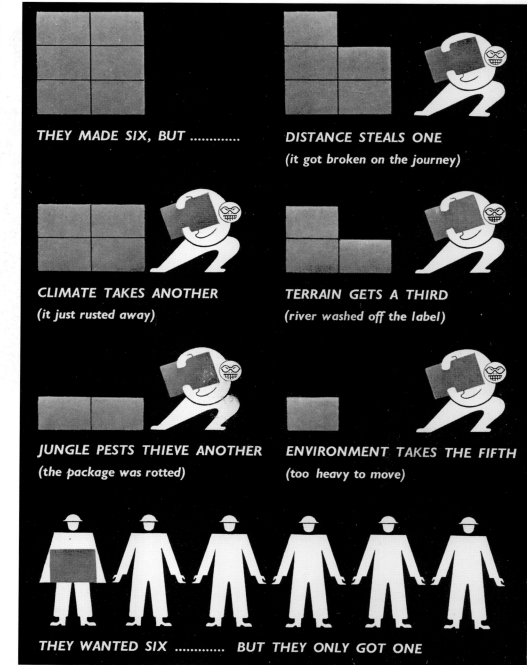

THEY MADE SIX, BUT ....

DISTANCE STEALS ONE
(it got broken on the journey)

CLIMATE TAKES ANOTHER
(it just rusted away)

TERRAIN GETS A THIRD
(river washed off the label)

JUNGLE PESTS THIEVE ANOTHER
(the package was rotted)

ENVIRONMENT TAKES THE FIFTH
(too heavy to move)

THEY WANTED SIX .... **BUT THEY ONLY GOT ONE**

Back at two o'clock.

I think it was Brigadier Denniston who observed that the account written of the RAOC performance on D-Day and beyond was academic as nothing would ever happen on that scale and in that way again. The same would have been true of a long land war against Japan.

It was also true that wars from now on would be on wheels and the RAOC had delivered. The British Army had successfully mechanised, and those who had enabled this had fought their war with distinction.

GLOSSARY

ABBREVIATIONS

AOD	Advance Ordnance Depot	MC	Military Cross
ATS	Auxiliary Territorial Service	MT	Motor Transport
BAD	Base Ammunition Depot	NCO	Non Commissioned Officer
BAS	British Army Staff	NCR	National Cash Registers
BEF	British Expeditionary Force	NMP	Nancy Mary Perks
BMP	Beach Maintenance Pack	OBD	Ordnance Beach Detachment
BOD	Base Ordnance Depot	OFP	Ordnance Field Park
CAD	Central Ammunition Depot	OTC	Officer Training Corps
CO	Commanding Officer	PLUTO	Pipeline Under The Sea
COD	Central Ordnance Depot	POW	Prisoner of War
COO	Chief Ordnance Officer	QMG	Quartermaster General
COS	Controller of Ordnance Services	RAOC	Royal Army Ordnance Corps
DCS	Director of Clothing and Stores	RASC	Royal Army Service Corps
DOS	Director of Ordnance Services	REME	Royal Electrical and Mechanical Engineers
FTS	Forward Trailer Section	RLC	Royal Logistics Corps
IBOD	Indian Base Ordnance Depot	SMMT	Society of Motor Manufacturers and Traders
IWM	Imperial War Museum	TK	Tel el Kebir
LAD	Light Aid Detachment	VRD	Vehicle Reserve Depot
LHW	Leslie Hamlyn Williams	VRS	Vehicle Reception Store
LR	Landing Reserve		

BIBLIOGRAPHY

80 Years of AEC, Townsin and Goulding, Senior Publications, Glossop, 1992

80 years of Guy Motors Limited, Hannay and Broatch, Venture, Glossop, 1994

A Complete Directory of Military Vehicles, Pat Ware, Southwater, Anness, Bournemouth, 2012

A summary of the transport used by the British Army 1939–1945, Conniford, MP, Bellona Publications 1969, pts I and II

An account of our stewardship being a record of the war-time activities of Vauxhall Motors Ltd, W.J. Seymour, Vauxhall Motors, Luton, 1946

Armoured Fighting Vehicles, Peter Griffin, Collins, Glasgow and London 1976

Austin Through the Years, The Austin Motor Company, Longbridge, 1962

Blood, Tears and Folly, Len Deighton, Cape, London, 1993

Bomber Boys: Fighting Back, 1940–45, Patrick Bishop, Kindle edn

Calling All Arms, Ernest Fairfax, Hutchinson, London, 1946

Drive for Freedom, Charles Graves, Hodder and Stoughton for the Society of Motor Maunfactuers and Traders

Dunkirk Inspiration: A Soldier's Story, Alwyn Ward, Sheffield, 1990 (RLC Archive)

Ford in the Service of America, Timothy J. O'Callaghan, McFarland & Co., 2009

General Motors: The First 75 Years of Transportation Products, Automobile Quarterly Publications, 1983

A History of the Royal Army Ordnance Corps 1920–1945, A.J. Fernihough, Royal Army Ordnance Corps, 1967

Overlord, D-Day and the Battle for Normandy 1944, Max Hastings, Book Club Associates, 1984

PLUTO: Pipe-Line Under the Ocean – The Definitive Story, Adrian Searle, Shanklin Chine, 1995

Task Tremendous Chilwell 1939–1945 (LHW papers)

The Chilwell Story (RLC Archive)

The Churchill Factor, Boris Johnson, Kindle edn

The Dunlop Story, James McMillan, Weidenfeld and Nicholson, 1989

The First Fifty Years, Leyland Motors Limited Leyland, Lancs 1946

The Illustrated History of Military Vehicles, Hogg and Weeks, Quarto Books, London, 1984

The Landships of Lincoln, Richard Pullen, Tucann, Lincoln, 2007

The Making of Modern Britain, Andrew Marr, MacMillan, Kindle edition

The Mulberry Harbour Project in Wigtownshire, A.T. Murchie, GC Book Publishers, Newton Stuart, 1999

The Rootes Brothers, Bullock, P. Stephens, Sparkford, 1993

The Second World War, Martin Gilbert, Phoenix, London, 1989, 2009

The Second World War, Parker, RAC, Oxford, 1989

The Story of an Enterprise 1885–1948, Oldham & Son Ltd, Manchester, 1948

The Tail of an Army, J.K. Stanford, Phoenix House, London, 1966

To the Warrior his Arms, Frank Steer, Pen and Sword, 2005

Wolseley: Saga of the Motor Industry, J.C. Nixon, Marshall Press, London, 1950

World War Two Tanks, George Forty, Osprey Automotive, London, 1995

NOTES

CHAPTER 1

1   *Drive for Freedom*, Charles Graves, p.4.
2   *History of the RAOC 1920–1945*, A.H. Fernyhough.
3   *History of the RAOC 1920–1945*, Fernyhough.
4   *Task Tremendous Chilwell 1939–1945*, unpublished.
5   *The Making of Modern Britain*, Andrew Marr.
6   *Drive for Freedom*, Charles Graves.
7   'The Chilwell Story', Royal Logistics Corps (RLC) archive, p. 82.
8   *Task Tremendous Chilwell 1939–1945*, Leslie 'Bill' Williams' (LHW) papers.
9   'The Chilwell Story', RLC archive, p. 83.
10 LHW's obituary of W.W. Richards, LHW papers.
11 NMP album.
12 *To the Warrior his Arms*, Frank Steer, p.1.
13 *History of the RAOC 1920–1945*, Fernyhough.
14 *To the Warrior his Arms*, Steer, p.16.
15 RLC archives, training box file.
16 NMP album 1.
17 NMP album 1.
18 *Overlord*, Max Hastings.
19 'The Chilwell Story', RLC archive.
20 'The Chilwell Story', RLC archive, p. 83.
21 'The Chilwell Story', RLC archive.
22 *History of the RAOC 1920–1945*, Fernyhough, p.41.
23 'The Chilwell Story', RLC archive, p. 83.
24 *The Rootes Brothers*, John Bullock.
25 LHW papers, Chilwell file.
26 Nancy Mary Williams' notes of LHW's recollections.
27 NMW notes of LHW's recollections.
28 'The Chilwell Story', RLC Archive, p. 91.
29 Newspaper cuttings from NMP album 1.
30 Address to RAOC press conference, 19 March 1942, NMP album 1.
31 LHW papers, Chilwell file.
32 NMP album.
33 Imperial War Museum (IWM) interview.
34 'The Chilwell Story', RLC archive.
35 M&S archives letter.

CHAPTER 2

1 *Calling All Arms*, Ernest Fairfax, p.5.
2 *Drive for Freedom*, Charles Graves, p.22.
3 *Drive for Freedom*, Charles Graves, p.29.
4 'Mobilisation of the Corps', RLC archive.
5 IWM recording.
6 IWM document, 3.11.14.
7 IWM document, 16.3.15.
8 IWM recording.
9 IWM recording.
10 *Dunkirk Inspiration*, Alwyn Ward.
11 IWM recording.
12 IWM recording.
13 IWM recording.
14 RLC archive.
15 Report on BEF, RLC archive.
16 *The Making of Modern Britain*, Andrew Marr.
17 *An account of our stewardship being a record of the war-time activities of Vauxhall Motors Ltd*, W.J. Seymour.
18 *The Illustrated History of Military Vehicles*, Hogg and Weeks, p.44.
19 NMP album.
20 RLC Museum.
21 *The Rootes Brothers*, John Bullock, p.33.
22 *The Rootes Brothers*, John Bullock, p.8.
23 *The Rootes Brothers*, John Bullock, p.83.
24 *The Rootes Brothers*, John Bullock, p.8.
25 *The Rootes Brothers*, John Bullock, p.127.
26 *The Rootes Brothers*, John Bullock, p.129.
27 *Calling all Arms*, Ernest Fairfax, p.15.
28 *The Rootes Brothers*, John Bullock, p.129.
29 *The Rootes Brothers*, John Bullock, p.130.
30 *The Rootes Brothers*, John Bullock, p.130.
31 *The Second World War*, Winston S. Churchill, Cassell, 1950, vol. IV, p.29.
32 *The Tank Story* brochure, The Tank Museum, Bovington.
33 *The Illustrated History of Military Vehicles*, Hogg and Weeks, p.18.
34 *The Illustrated History of Military Vehicles*, Hogg and Weeks, p.15.
35 *The Churchill Factor*, Boris Johnson.
36 *The Illustrated History of Military Vehicles*, Hogg and Weeks, p.28.
37 *The Illustrated History of Military Vehicles*, Hogg and Weeks, p.28.
38 *Calling all Arms*, Ernest Fairfax, p.48.
39 *Drive for Freedom*, Charles Graves, p.54.
40 *World War Two Tanks*, George Forty, p.54.
41 *World War Two Tanks*, George Forty, p.12.
42 *World War Two Tanks*, George Forty, p.40.
43 *World War Two Tanks*, George Forty, p.19.
44 Report on BEF, RLC archive.
45 Report on BEF, RLC archive.
46 *History of the RAOC 1920–1945*, Fernyhough, p.76.
47 *To the Warrior his Arms*, Frank Steer, p.66.
48 *The Tale of an Army*, J.K. Stanford, p.26.
49 *History of the RAOC 1920–1945*, Fernyhough, pp.88–89.
50 *History of the RAOC 1920–1945*, Fernyhough, p.80.
51 *History of the RAOC 1920–1945*, Fernyhough, p.78.
52 W.W. Richards papers, file 2, IWM.
53 *To the Warrior his Arms*, Frank Steer, p.68.
54 *To the Warrior his Arms*, Frank Steer, p.68.
55 *History of the RAOC 1920–1945*, Fernyhough, p.94.
56 IWM papers.
57 1st AA Brigade Workshop RAOC, Major G.S. Kellar, Lieutenant John A. Holman, Captain F. Fryer (IWM).
58 *Dunkirk Inspiration*, Alwyn Ward.
59 RLC archives.
60 *History of the RAOC 1920–1945*, Fernyhough, p.100.
61 *To the Warrior his Arms*, Frank Steer, p.70.
62 Author's interview with her granddaughter.
63 IWM recording.
64 IWM recording.
65 Report on BEF, RLC archive.

CHAPTER 3

1 National Motor Museum library.
2 *Drive for Freedom*, Charles Graves, p.43.
3 *History of the RAOC 1920–1945*, Fernyhough, p.85.
4 *Calling all Arms*, Fairfax, p.102.
5 *A Complete Directory of Military Vehicles*, Pat Ware, p.104.
6 *Austin Through the Years*, Austin Motor Company, 1962.
7 Author's meeting with fuel expert, Stuart Addy.
8 *Ford in the Service of America*, Timothy J. O'Callaghan, p.163.
9 *A Summary of the Transport Used by the British Army 1939–1945*, M.P. Conniford, Part 1, p.7.
10 *A Complete Directory of Military Vehicles*, Pat Ware, pp.110–1.
11 *A Complete Directory of Military Vehicles*, Pat Ware, p.122.
12 *Calling All Arms*, Fairfax, p.103.
13 *A Summary of the Transport Used by the British Army 1939–1945*, M.P. Conniford, Part 2, p.1.
14 *Wolseley, A Saga of the Motor Industry*, Nixon, p.117.
15 *Wolseley, A Saga of the Motor Industry*, Nixon, p.119.
16 *Wolseley, A Saga of the Motor Industry*, Nixon, p.139.
17 *A Complete Directory of Military Vehicles*, Pat Ware, p.106.
18 *A Complete Directory of Military Vehicles*, Pat Ware, p.107.
19 *Calling All Arms*, Fairfax, p.76.
20 *The Rootes Brothers*, John Bullock, p.69.
21 *A Complete Directory of Military Vehicles*, Pat Ware, p.113.
22 http://austin.tillyregister.com.
23 *Drive for Freedom*, Charles Graves, p.45.
24 *Calling all Arms*, Ernest Fairfax, p.81.
25 'Moonlight Sonata: the Coventry Blitz, 14/15 November 1940' by Tim Lewis and Coventry Council, 63, in *Bomber Boys: Fighting Back, 1940–45*, Patrick Bishop.
26 National Motor Museum display.
27 *Calling all Arms*, Ernest Fairfax, p.82.
28 *The Rootes Brothers*, John Bullock, p.131.
29 *80 Years of AEC*, Townsin and Goulding, p.33.
30 *A Summary of the Transport Used by the British Army 1939–1945*, M.P. Conniford, Part 2, p.1.
31 *A Complete Directory of Military Vehicles*, Pat Ware, p.99.
32 *A Summary of the Transport Used by the British Army 1939–1945*, Conniford, Part 2, p.15.
33 *A Summary of the Transport Used by the British Army 1939–1945*, Conniford, Part 2, p.15.
34 *A Complete Directory of Military Vehicles*, Pat Ware, p.101.
35 *A Summary of the Transport Used by the British Army 1939–1945*, Conniford, Part 1, p.1.
36 *Shepperton*, Crossley, Eyre, Heaps and Townsin, p.7.
37 *Shepperton*, Crossley, Eyre, Heaps and Townsin, p.82.
38 *80 years of Guy Motors Limited*, Hannay and Broatch, p.14.
39 *A Summary of the Transport Used by the British Army 1939–1945*, M.P. Conniford, Part 2, p.1.
40 *80 years of Guy Motors Limited*, Hannay and Broatch, p.45.
41 *80 years of Guy Motors Limited*, Hannay and Broatch, p.51.
42 *The Illustrated History of Military Vehicles*, Hogg and Weeks, p.49.
43 *A Complete Directory of Military Vehicles*, Pat Ware, p.119.
44 *A Summary of the Transport Used by the British Army 1939–1945*, Conniford, Part 1, p.16.
45 *Scammell*, Pat Kennett, Patrick Stephens, p.5.
46 *Scammell*, Pat Kennett, Patrick Stephens, p.6.
47 *Scammell*, Pat Kennett, Patrick Stephens, p.32; *A Complete Directory of Military Vehicles*, Pat Ware, pp.124–5.
48 *A Summary of the Transport Used by the British Army 1939–1945*, Conniford, Part 1, p.7.
49 *Scammell*, Pat Kennett, Patrick Stephens, p.26.
50 *Task Tremendous Chilwell 1939–1945*.
51 *The Dunlop Story*, James McMillan, p.79.
52 *The Story of an Enterprise 1885–1948*.
53 *Drive for Freedom*, Charles Graves, p.89.
54 *Armoured Fighting Vehicles*, Peter Griffin, p.40.
55 *World War Two Tanks*, George Forty, p.44.
56 *Armoured Fighting Vehicles*, Peter Griffin, p.40.
57 *World War Two Tanks*, George Forty, p.12.
58 *The First Fifty Years, Leyland Motors Limited*, Leyland Motors, p.64.
59 *Task Tremendous Chilwell 1939–1945*.
60 *An account of our stewardship being a record of the war-time activities of Vauxhall Motors Ltd*, W.J. Seymour.
61 *Armoured Fighting Vehicles*, Peter Griffin, p.41.
62 *World War Two Tanks*, George Forty, p.49.
63 *Task Tremendous Chilwell 1939–1945*, p.20.

CHAPTER 4

1 NMP album.
2 IWM recording.
3 *The Tale of an Army*, J.K. Stanford.
4 *RAOC Gazette*, September 1965.
5 *The Making of Modern Britain*, Andrew Marr.
6 NMP album, Carmen speech.
7 NMP album.
8 De Wolff memoir, RLC archive.
9 Author's correspondence with veteran.
10 Phone call responding to request in local newspaper.
11 De Wolff memoir, RLC archive.
12 NMP album.
13 De Wolff memoir, RLC archive.
14 De Wolff memoir, RLC archive.
15 NMP album.
16 LHW papers.
17 IWM recording.
18 NMP album.
19 NMP album 2.
20 *History of the RAOC 1920–1945*, Fernyhough, p.446.
21 NMP album.
22 NMP album 2.
23 NMP album 2.
24 NMP album.
25 NMP album.
26 NMP album.
27 Email in response to a request in newspaper.
28 NMP album.
29 *Task Tremendous Chilwell 1939–1945*.
30 RLC archive.
31 NMP album 2.
32 NMW album 2.
33 RLC archive.
34 RLC archive.
35 LHW papers.
36 'The Chilwell Story', RLC archive, p. 101.
37 DVD from her son, Tony Steer.
38 NMP album.
39 RLC archive.
40 RLC archive.
41 RLC archive and NMP album.
42 War diary 1943, held at The National Archives.
43 Phone conversation in response to newspaper request.
44 De Wolff memoirs, RLC archive.
45 *A Kind of Soldiering*, Howard Palmer.
46 The National Archives.
47 *History of the RAOC 1920–1945*, Fernyhough, p.362 and www.thepeerage.com/p7951.htm#i79503.
48 *History of the RAOC 1920–1945*, Fernyhough, p.441.
49 NMP album.

CHAPTER 5

1 W.W. Richards papers, IWM.
2 W.W. Richards papers, IWM.
3 *History of the RAOC 1920–1945*, Fernyhough, p.172.
4 W.W. Richards papers, IWM.
5 *History of the RAOC 1920–1945*, Fernyhough, p.206.
6 *Blood, Tears and Folly*, Len Deighton.
7 W.W. Richards papers, IWM.
8 W.W. Richards papers, IWM.
9 *The Second World War*, Parker, p.98.
10 *The Second World War*, Parker, p.98.
11 *To the Warrior his Arms*, Frank Steer, p.75.
12 *To the Warrior his Arms*, Frank Steer, p.78.
13 RLC archive.
14 *To the Warrior his Arms*, Frank Steer, p.79.
15 W.W. Richards papers, IWM.
16 W.W. Richards papers, IWM.

17 *The Dunlop Story*, James McMillan, p.78.

18 *Calling all Arms*, Ernest Fairfax, p.54.

19 *Drive for Freedom*, Charles Graves, p.54.

20 *Calling all Arms*, Ernest Fairfax, p.61.

21 The National Archives.

22 *Overlord*, Max Hastings.

23 Facebook message to author.

24 Story told face to face with author.

25 *The Second World War*, Winston Churchill, Vol. III, p.777.

26 W.W. Richards papers, IWM.

27 IWM recording.

28 NMP album.

29 IWM recording.

30 RLC archive.

31 The National Archives.

32 NMP album.

33 IWM papers.

34 *History of the RAOC 1920–1945*, Fernyhough.

CHAPTER 6

1   LHW papers, 21 Army Group Ordnance.

2   *History of the RAOC 1920–1945*, Fernyhough, p.363.

3   *PLUTO: Pipe-Line Under the Ocean*, Adrian Searle.

4   *The Mulberry Harbour Project in Wigtownshire*, A.T. Murchie, p.9.

5   *The Mulberry Harbour Project in Wigtownshire*, A.T. Murchie.

6   NMP album.

7   RLC archive.

8   RLC archive.

9   NMP album.

10 RLC archive.

11 RLC archive.

12 NMP album.

13 RLC archive.

14 *Task Tremendous Chilwell 1939–1945*.

15 LHW papers, 21 Army Group Ordnance.

16 NMP album.

17 NMP album.

18 *The Rootes Brothers*, John Bullock, p.134.

19 NMP album.

20 *To the Warrior his Arms*, Frank Steer, p.98.

21 NMP album.

22 LHW papers, report on visit.

23 LHW papers, report on visit.

24 *Ford in the Service of America*, Timothy J. O'Callaghan, p.35.

25 *Ford in the Service of America*, Timothy J. O'Callaghan, p.36.

26 *Ford in the Service of America*, Timothy J. O'Callaghan, p.127.

27 *Ford in the Service of America*, Timothy J. O'Callaghan, p.130.

28 *Ford in the Service of America*, Timothy J. O'Callaghan, p.115.

29 *Ford in the Service of America*, Timothy J. O'Callaghan, p.113.

30 *Ford in the Service of America*, Timothy J. O'Callaghan, p.162.

31 *General Motors, The First 75 years of Transportation Products*, General Motors, pp.108–9.

32 NMP album.

33 NMP album.

34 LHW papers.

35 LHW papers.

36 NMP album.

37 LHW papers.

38 LHW papers.

39 LHW papers.

40 *Calling all Arms*, Ernest Fairfax, p.61.

41 NMP album 2.

42 *Overlord*, Max Hastings, p.103.

43 *The British Soldier From D-Day to VE Day*, Vol. 2, 'Organisation, Armament, Tanks and Vehicles', Jean Bouchery, translated by Alan McKay, Histoire & Collections, Paris.

44 *Task Tremendous Chilwell 1939–1945*.

45 IWM interview.

46 *Overlord*, Max Hastings.

CHAPTER 7

1 IWM recording.
2 RLC archive.
3 RLC archive.
4 LHW papers, 21 Army Group Ordnance.
5 IWM recording.
6 The National Archives.
7 LHW papers, 21 Army Group Ordnance.
8 LHW papers, 21 Army Group Ordnance.
9 Face-to-face interview.
10 NMP album.
11 *Overlord*, Max Hastings, p.198.
12 *Overlord*, Max Hastings, p.201.
13 IWM recording.
14 *PLUTO: Pipe-Line Under the Ocean*, Adrian Searle.
15 RLC archive.
16 IWM interview.
17 LHW papers, 15 and 17 AOD.
18 LHW papers, 21 Army Group Ordnance.
19 LHW papers, 21 Army Group Ordnance.
20 LHW papers, 21 Army Group Ordnance.
21 IWM interview.
22 *Calling all Arms*, Ernest Fairfax, 64.
23 RLC archive.
24 IWM interview.
25 IWM recording.

CHAPTER 8

1 *History of the RAOC 1920–1945*, Fernyhough, p.308.
2 History of the RAOC 1920–1945, Fernyhough, p.320.
3 IWM recording.
4 IWM, P.R. Barroud (private papers).
5 IWM recording.
6 IWM recording.
7 IWM recording.
8 IWM private papers.
9 IWM private papers.
10 IWM private papers.
11 National Army Museum private papers.
12 LHW papers.
13 LHW papers.
14 NMP album.
15 LHW papers.
16 LHW papers.

You might also be interested in …

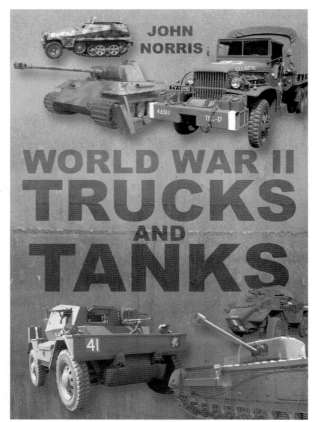

978 0 7509 6602 6

From jeeps to tanks, landrovers to ambulances, this is
the perfect book for recreating, restoring and exploring
the history of these vehicles that were vital to the
war effort.

The destination for history
www.thehistorypress.co.uk